Contemporary's
NUMBER POWER
Word Problems

KENNETH TAMARKIN

Consultants:
Michael Dean
Elizabeth Shaw
VTAE—Adult H.S. Program
Broward County, Florida

Project Editor:
Caren Van Slyke

Contemporary Books, Inc.
Chicago

Published by Contemporary Books, Inc.
180 North Michigan Avenue, Chicago, Illinois 60601
Manufactured in the United States of America
International Standard Book Number: 0-8092-5750-5

Published simultaneously in Canada by Beaverbooks, Ltd.
195 Allstate Parkway, Valleywood Business Park
Markham, Ontario L3R 4T8 Canada

Production Editor: Gerry Lynch
Illustrations: Louise Hodges

TABLE OF CONTENTS

TO THE STUDENT

Word problems are an important part of your study of mathematics. You find them on many educational and vocational tests, in your studies, and at your work. Most math texts carefully explain how to arrive at solutions, but too often they do not devote any effort to helping students work with word problems.

NUMBER POWER 6: WORD PROBLEMS is a different type of math book. It is totally devoted to helping you understand and solve word problems. The book has been carefully organized so that you can proceed step-by-step from relatively simple to very complicated problems.

Chapter 1 introduces you to word problems. Chapters 2-4 are concerned with problems involving addition or subtraction of whole numbers, fractions, and decimals. Chapters 5-7 discuss multiplication and division. Operations have been paired together to help you develop your comprehension of the problems. Chapter 8 allows you to review what you have learned.

Chapters 9 and 10 concern two areas that often give students problems. Chapter 9 is devoted to solving percent-related problems and Chapter 10 helps you figure out how to solve a problem that combines several operations. The final section allows you to see how well you have mastered word problems.

As you work through this book, your understanding and abilities with word problems will grow. We hope that NUMBER POWER 6 will become a book that you will work through carefully and return to again and again to sharpen your mathematical and problem-solving abilities.

CHAPTER 1:
Introduction To Word Problems

WHAT ARE WORD PROBLEMS?

A word problem is a sentence or group of sentences that tell a story, contain numbers, and ask the reader to find another number.

This is an example of a word problem:

> Last week, Paula earned $94. The week before, she earned $88. What was the total amount of money she earned?

STEPS IN SOLVING WORD PROBLEMS

In this book, you will use 5 steps to solve word problems. It is important to follow these steps to organize your thinking. They will help you figure out what may seem to be a difficult puzzle. In all cases, read the problem carefully, more than once if necessary. Then follow these steps.

Step 1: First, determine what the *question* is asking you to find.

Step 2: Then, decide what *information* is *necessary* in order to solve the problem.

Step 3: Next, decide what *arithmetic operation* to use.

Step 4: Work out the problem and find the solution. Check your arithmetic. This isn't the last step . . .

Step 5: *Reread the question* to make sure that your answer *is sensible.*

Many people can do some word problems "in their heads." This is known as *math intuition* and works well with small whole numbers. This intuition often breaks down with larger numbers, decimals, and especially fractions. Additionally, word problems of two or more steps can be even more difficult.

You should practice the 5-step approach even with problems that you could solve "in your head." Then you will have something to fall back on when intuition is not enough.

STEP 1:   THE QUESTION

After reading a word problem, the first step in solving it is to decide what is being asked for. You must find the question.

The following word problem consists of only one sentence. This sentence asks a question and contains the information that is needed to solve the problem.

Example 1:   How much did Mel spend on dinner when the food cost $20 and the tax was $1?

The question asks, "How much did Mel spend on dinner?"

The next word problem contains two sentences. One sentence asks the question and the other sentence gives the information that is necessary to solve the problem.

Example 2:   Mary got $67 a month in food stamps for 9 months. What was the total value of the stamps?

The question asks, "What was the total value of the stamps?"

Example 3 also contains two sentences. Notice that *both* sentences contain information that is necessary to solve the problem.

Example 3:   The Little Sweetheart Tea Set normally costs $8.95. How much did Alice save by buying the tea set for her daughter at an after-Christmas sale for $5.49?

The question asks, "How much did Alice save?"

EXERCISE 1:   Underline the question in each of the following word problems. DO NOT SOLVE!!

1. Last winter, it snowed 5 inches in December, 17 inches in January, 13 inches in February, and 2 inches in March. How much snow fell during the entire winter?

2. In order to cook the chicken, first brown it for 10 minutes. Then lower the temperature and let it simmer for 20 more minutes. What is the total cooking time?

3. How much does it cost to park at the meter for 3 hours if it costs 25 cents an hour to park?

4. How many years did Joe serve in prison if his sentence of five years was reduced by three for good behavior?

Answers on page 143.

STEP 2: SELECTING THE NECESSARY INFORMATION

After finding the question, the next step in solving a word problem is *selecting the necessary information*. The necessary information consists of the *numbers* and the *labels* (words or symbols) that go with the numbers. The necessary information includes *only* the numbers and labels that you need to solve the problem.

The labels make the numbers in word problems concrete. For example, the necessary information in Example 1 below is not just the number 5, but includes 5 apples. Paying close attention to labels will help you learn many of the methods shown in this book and will help you avoid common mistakes with word problems.

After each of the following examples, the necessary information is listed.

Example 1:   Doreen bought 5 apples last week and 6 apples this week. How many apples did she buy altogether?

The necessary information is 5 apples and 6 apples. Both numbers are followed by the label word "apples."

Example 2:   A shirt costs $9.99. What is the cost of 5 shirts?

The necessary information is $9.99 and 5 shirts. The labels are the dollar sign ($) and the word "shirts."

EXERCISE 2: In each word problem, find the necessary information. Circle the numbers and underline the labels. Then, on the line provided, write the label that would be a part of the answer, but DO NOT SOLVE!!

1. On Friday, a commuter train took 124 commuters to work and 119 commuters home. How many commuters rode the train that day?

   _____

2. 7 waitresses had equal responsibility for the 56 tables in John's Diner. How many tables did each waitress have to wait on?

   _____

3. Unleaded gasoline costs 6 cents more per gallon than regular. Regular costs $1.47 a gallon. How much does unleaded gasoline cost?

   _____

4. The radio station added $38 more to the $329 already in the superjackpot. What is the new amount of money in the superjackpot?

   _____

5. A chair has 4 legs. How many legs must a carpenter make for a set of 6 chairs?

   _____

Answers on page 143.

NECESSARY VS. GIVEN INFORMATION

Sometimes a word problem contains numbers that aren't needed to answer the question. You must read problems carefully to choose only the necessary information.

Notice this important difference: The *given information* includes *all* of the numbers and labels in a word problem.

The *necessary information* includes *only* those numbers and labels needed to solve the problem.

Example 1: Nelson travels to and from work with 3 friends every day. The round trip is 9 miles. If he works 5 days a week, how many miles does he commute in a week?

given information: 3 friends, 9 miles, 5 days
necessary information: 9 miles, 5 days

In order to figure out how many miles he commutes in a week, you do not need to know that Nelson travels with 3 friends.

Example 2: There are 7,000 people living in Dry Gulch. Of the 3,000 people who are registered to vote, only 1,700 people participated in the last election. How many registered voters did not vote?

given information: 7,000 people, 3,000 people, 1,700 people
necessary information: 3,000 people, 1,700 people

This type of word problem containing unnecessary information may be a little tricky. All of the numbers have the same label—people. However, careful reading of the problem shows that the total number of people in the town (7,000), is not needed to figure out the number of registered voters who did not vote.

As you work through the problems in this and other books, watch out for problems containing unnecessary numbers and labels.

EXERCISE 3: This exercise will help you tell the difference between given and necessary information. Underline the given information. Circle the necessary information. DO NOT SOLVE!

1. Mona is 22 years old. She has a sister who is 20 years old and a boyfriend who is 23. How much older is Mona than her sister?

2. Rena receives $86 a month from the AFDC aid program. She also receives $67 a month in food stamps in order to help feed her 2 children. How much public assistance does she receive each month?

3. Marilyn works three times as many hours as her 20-year-old sister Laura. Laura works 10 hours a week. How many hours a week does Marilyn work?

4. Suzanne spent $43 on gasoline last month for her 7-year-old car. This month she has spent $39. How much did she spend on gasoline during the 2 months?

5. During the winter, the Right Foot Shoe Store spent $2,460 for oil heat and sold $35,800 worth of shoes. If oil cost $1.20 per gallon, how many gallons did the shoe store buy?

6. Erma, who is 45, cooks dinner for the 8 people in her family. Her husband, Jack, cooks breakfast in the mornings for only half of the family. For how many people does Jack cook?

7. In a factory of 4,700 workers, 3,900 are skilled laborers. 700 of the employees are on layoff. How many people are currently working?

Answers on page 143.

CHAPTER 2:
Addition and Subtraction Word Problems: Whole Numbers

In Chapter 1, you worked on finding the question and the necessary information in a word problem. The third step in solving a word problem is *deciding which arithmetic operation to use*.

In Chapters 2, 3, and 4, you will be looking at word problems that can be solved by using either addition or subtraction. You will learn four methods that can be used to decide whether to add or subtract. These methods are:

> **1.** finding the key words
> **2.** restating the problem
> **3.** making drawings and diagrams
> **4.** writing number sentences

You will also work with making estimates and substitutions.

All of these methods are useful in understanding and solving word problems. After learning them, you may decide to use one or more of the methods that you find most helpful.

FINDING ADDITION KEY WORDS

How do you know that you must add to solve a word problem? Key words can be helpful. A key word is a clue that can help you decide which arithmetic to use.

Note: "How many," "how much," and "what" are general mathematics question words, but they are not key words. They help to identify the question, but do not tell you whether to add, subtract, multiply, or divide.

The following examples contain addition key words.

Example 1: What is the sum of 3 dollars and 2 dollars?

addition key words: sum, and

The sum is the answer to an addition problem. Therefore, when the word "sum" appears in a word problem, it is a clue that you should probably add to solve the problem.

Example 2: The small cup contains 16 ounces of soda. The large size contains 6 more ounces. How many ounces are in the large size cup?

addition key word: more

The word "more" suggests that you should add the two amounts together.

EXERCISE 1:   In the following exercise, circle the key words that suggest addition. DO NOT SOLVE!!

1. Karen bought a new car for $5,640 plus $460 for options. How much did she spend for the car?

2. Judy bought four lemons and twelve oranges. How many pieces of fruit did she buy altogether?

3. What is the sum of 5 chairs and 7 chairs?

4. A recipe for pumpkin pie says that an extra 2 tablespoons of sugar can be added for extra sweetness. The standard recipe calls for 4 tablespoons of sugar. How many tablespoons of sugar are needed for the sweeter pie?

5. The price of a $3 general admission ticket to the ballpark will increase $1 next year. What will be the general admission price next year?

6. Although she has lost 15 pounds, Pam wants to lose 10 more. How much weight does she want to lose altogether?

Answers on page 143.

SOLVING ADDITION WORD PROBLEMS WITH KEY WORDS

You have now looked at the first three steps in solving a word problem:

Step 1: Finding the question
Step 2: Selecting the necessary information
Step 3: Deciding what arithmetic to use

The next step in solving a word problem is doing the arithmetic. People who have not learned to think carefully about word problems may rush into doing the arithmetic and become confused. However, the three steps before doing the arithmetic and the one step after provide a good way to organize your thinking to solve a problem. The actual arithmetic is only one of several necessary steps.

Look again at Example 1 from the "Finding Addition Key Words" section:

What is the sum of 3 dollars and 2 dollars?

Step 1:	*the question:* What is the sum?
Step 2:	*necessary information:* 3 dollars, 2 dollars
Step 3:	*addition key words:* sum, and
Step 4:	*add:* 3 dollars + 2 dollars = **5 dollars**

$$\begin{array}{r} 3 \\ +2 \\ \hline 5 \end{array}$$

Now look at Example 2:

The small size cup contains 16 ounces of soda. The large size contains 6 more ounces. How many ounces are in the large size cup?

Step 1:	*the question:* How many ounces are in the large size cup?
Step 2:	*necessary information:* 16 ounces, 6 ounces
Step 3:	*addition key word:* more
Step 4:	*add:* 16 ounces + 6 ounces = **22 ounces**

$$\begin{array}{r} 16 \\ +6 \\ \hline 22 \end{array}$$

Once you have completed the arithmetic there is one last step. Reread the question and make sure that the answer is sensible.

For instance in Example 2, if you had subtracted, you would have gotten an answer of 10 ounces. Would it have made sense to say that the larger size was 10 ounces?

EXERCISE 2: This exercise contains one-sentence word problems with key words. For each problem, circle the key word or words and do the arithmetic. Write the answer on the line below the problem. Be sure to include the label as part of your answer.

1. After 5 inches of snow fell on a base of 23 inches of snow, how many inches of snow were on the ski trail altogether?

   _____

2. What was the new bus fare in the five-county area after the fare of 50 cents was increased by 20 cents?

   _____

3. What is the total weight of a 3,500-pound truck carrying a 720-pound load?

   _____

4. How big an apartment is the Dao family looking for if they want one that is two rooms larger than their three-room apartment?

_____

5. After raising $121,460 the first year and $89,742 the second, how much money was in the church building fund?

_____

Answers on page 143.

FINDING SUBTRACTION KEY WORDS

Each of the key words in Exercises 1 and 2 helped you decide to add. Other key words may help you decide to subtract. Here is an example of a word problem using subtraction key words:

Example 1: What is the difference between 3 dollars and 2 dollars?

Step 1: *the question:* What is the difference?

Step 2: *necessary information:* 3 dollars, 2 dollars

Step 3: *subtracton key words:* difference between

The necessary information, 3 dollars and 2 dollars, is the same as in the first addition key word example. However, in this example, the key words "difference between" are subtraction key words. To find the difference means to subtract.

Example 2: The large size cup contains 16 ounces of soda. The small size contains 6 ounces less than the large cup. How may ounces does the small cup contain?

Step 1: *the question:* How many ounces does the small cup contain?

Step 2: *necessary information:* 16 ounces, 6 ounces

Step 3: *subtraction key words:* less than

Note: In some subtraction word problems, the key words "less" and "than" are separated by other words. This is also true for "more" and "than."

EXERCISE 3:   In the following exercise, circle the key words that suggest subtraction. DO NOT SOLVE!

1. Bargain Air Lines is $25 cheaper than First Class Air. First Class charges $100 for a flight from Kansas City to St. Louis. What does Bargain Air Lines charge?

2. Out of 7,103 students, State College had 1,423 graduates last year. This year there were 1,251 graduates. What was the decrease in the number of graduates?

3. The large size steak weighs 12 ounces. The small size weighs 5 ounces less. How much does the small size weigh?

4. The large engine has 258 horsepower. The economy engine has 92 horsepower. What is the difference in horsepower between the two engines?

5. This year Great Rapids has 15 schools. Next year the number of schools will be reduced by 2. How many schools does the city plan to open next year?

Answers on page 143.

SOLVING SUBTRACTION WORD PROBLEMS WITH KEY WORDS

You can now complete Example 1 of the "Finding Subtraction Key Words" section:

What is the difference between 3 dollars and 2 dollars?

Step 1:	*the question:* What is the difference?
Step 2:	*necessary information:* 3 dollars, 2 dollars
Step 3:	*subtraction key words:* difference
Step 4:	*subtract:* 3 dollars − 2 dollars = **1 dollar**

$$\begin{array}{r} 3 \\ -2 \\ \hline 1 \end{array}$$

Now, look at Example 2:

The large size cup contains 16 ounces of soda. The small size contains 6 ounces less than the large cup. How many ounces does the small size cup contain?

Step 1: *the question:* How many ounces are in the small size cup?

Step 2: *necessary information:* 16 ounces, 6 ounces

Step 3: *subtraction key words:* less than

Step 4: *subtract:* 16 ounces − 6 ounces = **10 ounces**

$$\begin{array}{r} 16 \\ -\ 6 \\ \hline 10 \end{array}$$

Example 3: How much less does a $13 polyester dress cost than a $24 cotton one?

Step 1: *the question:* How much less does a $13 polyester dress cost?

Step 2: *necessary information:* $13, $24

Step 3: *subtraction key words:* less than

Step 4: *subtract:* $24 − $13 = **$11**

$$\begin{array}{r} 24 \\ -13 \\ \hline 11 \end{array}$$

In example 3, the key words "less" and "than" are separated.

This is also an example of a common type of subtraction problem. In order to solve it, you must reverse the order in which the numbers appear in the problem.

EXERCISE 4: In each problem below, circle the key words and do the arithmetic.

1. After a tornado destroyed 36 of the 105 homes in Carson, how many homes were left?

    _____

2. How much change did Mel receive when he paid for $16 worth of gas with a $20 bill?

    _____

3. After spending $325 of the $361 in her savings
    account for Christmas presents, how much did
    Carmena have left in her account?

    _____

4. What is the difference in price between a $12,635
    Cadillac and a $7,849 Dodge?

    _____

5. The temperature has fallen 12 degrees from the
    afternoon high of 86 degrees, following a morning
    low of 58 degrees. What is the evening tempera-
    ture?

    _____

Answers on page 143.

_____

ADDITION AND SUBTRACTION KEY WORD LISTS

Now you know that some key words may help you decide to add. Other
key words may help you decide to subtract.

Here are some important key words to remember:

Addition Key Words
Sum
Plus
Add
And
Total
Increase
More
Raise
Both
Combined
In all
Altogether
Additional

You may want to add more words to this list

Subtraction Key Words
Less than
More than
Decrease
Difference
Reduce
Lost
Left
Remain
Fell
Dropped
Change
Nearer } other -er comparison words
Farther }

You may want to add more words to this list.

SOLVING ONE-SENTENCE WORD PROBLEMS WITH KEY WORDS

The one-sentence word problem is often the least complicated type of word problem. It usually states directly what to look for, and contains few, if any, unnecessary facts.

EXERCISE 5:   In the following set of one-sentence word problems, circle the key words. On the first line after each problem, write "add" if you must add to solve the problem or "subtract" if you must subtract to solve it. Finally, solve the problem and write the answer on the second line.

1. How many cans did Diane buy in all if she bought 5 cans of peas, 3 bags of potatoes, and 8 cans of tomatoes?

   _____

   _____

2. How much more does a 26-pound dog weigh than a 12-pound dog?

   _____

   _____

3. What was the total inventory of white paint at the hardware store after the shipment of 23 cans was added to the stock of 57 cans?

   _____

   _____

4. How much will a 3,900-pound elephant weigh after gaining 240 pounds?

_____

_____

5. What is the cost of a $345 suit after the price had been reduced by $68?

_____

_____

6. How much longer is a 262-foot jet than a 38-foot private plane?

_____

_____

Answers on page 144.

___

SOLVING ADDITION AND SUBTRACTION PROBLEMS WITH KEY WORDS

Up to now, you have mainly worked with one-sentence word problems. But most word problems are more than one sentence long. In this section, you will look at word problems containing two or more sentences.

Example 1: It snowed 7 inches on Monday and 5 inches on Friday. What was the total amount of snow for the week?

Step 1: *the question:* What is the total amount of snow?

Step 2: *necessary information:* 7 inches, 5 inches

Step 3: *addition key words:* and, total

Step 4: *add:* 7 inches + 5 inches = **12 inches.**

$$\begin{array}{r} 7 \\ +5 \\ \hline 12 \end{array}$$

Example 2: The city usually runs its entire fleet of 237 buses during the morning rush hour. On Thursday morning, 46 buses and 13 subway cars were out of service. How many buses were left to run during the Thursday morning rush hour?

Step 1: *the question:* How many buses were running Thursday morning?

Step 2: *necessary information:* 237 buses, 46 buses (13 subway cars is not necessary information.)

Step 3: *subtraction key word:* left

Step 4: *subtract:* 237 buses − 46 buses = **191 buses.**

$$\begin{array}{r} 237 \\ -46 \\ \hline 191 \end{array}$$

EXERCISE 6:   In this exercise, circle the key words. Decide whether to add or to subtract. Then solve the problem, and write the answer on the line below.

1. A book saleswoman sold 86 books on Monday and 53 books on Tuesday. How many books did she sell altogether?

   _____

2. After selling 15 rings on Wednesday, a jeweler sold 31 rings and 4 necklaces on Thursday. How many more rings did she sell on Thursday than on Wednesday?

   _____

3. At a town meeting, 564 people voted "yes" on the budget and 365 voted "no." What was the total vote on the budget?

   _____

4. This year the Graphics Computer Company sold 253 units. Last year it sold 421 units. By how many units did sales decrease this year?

   _____

5. Mammoth Oil advertises that with its new brand of oil, a car can drive 10,000 miles between oil changes. Their other oil had to be changed every 3,000 miles. How much farther can you drive with Mammoth's new oil than with their old oil?

   _____

6. Last year, the Gonzales family paid $230 a month rent. If their rent was increased by $35 a month, how much monthly rent are they now paying?

   _____

Answers on page 144.

CHAPTER 3:
More Addition And Subtraction Word Problems: Whole Numbers

KEY WORDS CAN BE MISLEADING

You now know that there are five steps in solving a word problem:

Step 1:	Finding the question
Step 2:	Selecting the necessary information
Step 3:	Deciding what arithmetic to use
Step 4:	Finding the solution
Step 5:	Making sure that the answer is sensible

Most of this book is devoted to helping you with Step 3—deciding what arithmetic to use. So far you have seen one approach:

1. Find the key word.
2. Decide whether the key word suggests addition or subtraction.
3. Do the arithmetic the key word directs you to do.

This approach can work in many situations.

But Be Careful!

Sometimes the same key word that helped you decide to add in one word problem can also appear in a problem that requires subtraction.

The next two examples use the *same* numbers and the *same* key words. In one problem, you must add to find the answer, while in the other, you must subtract.

Example 1: Judy bought 4 cans of pineapple and 16 cans of applesauce. What was the total number of cans that she bought?

Step 1: *question:* What was the total amount of cans?

Step 2: *necessary information:* 4 cans of pineapple, 16 cans of applesauce

Step 3: *key words:* and, total
Since you are looking for a total, you should add.

Step 4: 4 cans of pineapple + 16 cans of applesauce = **20 cans of fruit**

$$\begin{array}{r} 16 \\ +4 \\ \hline 20 \end{array}$$

Example 2:   Judy bought a total of 16 cans of fruit. 4 were cans of pineapple. The rest were applesauce. How many cans of applesauce did she buy?

Step 1:   *question:* How many cans of applesauce did she buy?

Step 2:   *necessary information:* 4 cans of pineapple, 16 cans of fruit

Step 3:   *key word:* total

Since you have been given a total and are being asked to find a part of it, you must subtract.

Step 4:   16 cans of fruit − 4 cans of pineapple = **12 cans of applesauce**

$$\begin{array}{r} 16 \\ -\ 4 \\ \hline 12 \end{array}$$

In both examples, the word "total" was used. In Example 1, the question asked you to find the total. Therefore, you had to add.

But in Example 2, the total (cans of fruit) was part of the information given in the problem. The question asked you to find the number of cans of applesauce, a part of the total. To do this, you had to subtract the number of cans of pineapple from the total number of cans.

These two examples show that key words can be good clues, <u>but they are only a guide to understanding a word problem.</u> If you use key words without understanding what you are reading, you may do the wrong arithmetic.

EXERCISE 1:   This exercise will help you to carefully examine problems containing key words. In each of the following items, the key word has been left out and the solution has been given. Two choices have been given for the missing word; circle the correct one.

1.   Last week eggs cost 87 cents a dozen. This week the price _____ 9 cents. How much are eggs this week?

87 cents + 9 cents = **96 cents**

(fell, rose)

2.   Last week the price of eggs _____ to 87 cents a dozen. The price had originally been 78 cents. By how much did the eggs change in price?

87 cents − 78 cents = **9 cents**

(fell, rose)

3.   The 5% sales tax is going to _____ 1%. What will the new sales tax be?

5% + 1% = **6%**

(increase, decrease)

4. The 5% sales tax is going to _____ 1%. What will the new sales tax be?

5% − 1% = **4%**

(increase, decrease)

5. Next month, the Jones family is going to receive $14 a week _____ for food stamps. They now receive $87 a week. How much a week will they be receiving?

$87 − $14 = **$73**

(more, less)

6. The Johnson family's food stamp allotment has been cut. They now receive $14 a month _____, or $87 for stamps. What had been their original allotment for stamps?

$87 + $14 = **$101**

(more, less)

7. Gloria used to keep her thermostat at 72 degrees. To save energy, she _____ it 6 degrees. What was the new temperature of her apartment?

72 degrees − 6 degrees = **66 degrees**

(raised, lowered)

8. Jerline's mother came to visit for the weekend. To make sure that her mother was comfortable, she _____ the thermostat to 72 degrees. Usually, the thermostat is set at 66 degrees. By how much has Jerline changed the temperature?

72 degrees − 66 degrees = **6 degrees**

(lowered, raised)

9. Gail normally ate 2,400 calories a day. While on a special diet, she ate 1,100 calories _____. How many calories a day did she eat on her diet?

2,400 calories + 1,100 calories = **3,500 calories**

(more, less)

Answers on page 144.

In order to understand and work out word problems, people try to "get a picture" of the problem. This can be done in many ways. The next two methods, restating the problem and drawing a diagram or picture, are methods that you can develop in ways that suit you best. The following exercises show ways to use these two approaches.

RESTATING A PROBLEM

Have you ever tried to help someone else work out a word problem? Think about what you do. Often, you read the problem with the person and then discuss it or put it in your own words to help them see what is happening. This method, restating the problem, can be done on your own as a form of "talking to yourself."

Try this method with Exercise 2 below. Read the problem and then restate it to yourself. Below the problems are the types of explanations that a person might give to himself about whether to add or subtract. In future work, you should try this method of "talking to yourself" to understand a particularly confusing word problem.

EXERCISE 2:   Each word problem is followed by two short explanations. One gives you a reason to add to find the answer. The other gives you a reason to subtract to find the answer. Put an "X" next to the letter of the correct explanation. DO NOT SOLVE!

1. Margi's weekly food budget has increased $12 over last year's to $57 per week. How much had she spent for food last year?

_____A.   *The budget has increased since last year. Therefore you must add the two numbers.*

_____B.   *Her food budget has increased over last year's. The new, larger budget is given. Therefore you must subtract to find last year's smaller amount.*

2. In the final run-off election for mayor, Fritz Neptune got 14,662 votes and Julio Cortez got 17,139 votes. How many votes were cast in the election?

_____A.   *In order to find the total number of votes cast, you should add the two numbers given.*

_____B.   *In order to find the number of votes cast, you should subtract to find the difference between the two numbers.*

3. The difference between first class (the most expen-
    sive fare) and the coach air fare is $68. If coach
    costs $112, how much does first class cost?

    _____A. *To find the cost of first class, you must
             subtract to find the difference between
             the two fares.*

    _____B. *First class costs more than coach.
             Since you are looking for the larger
             fare, you must add the smaller fare to
             the difference between the two.*

4. It costs $36,840 to run and maintain the town's
    pool. During the year, $19,176 was collected from
    user fees for the pool, and the town government
    paid the rest of the cost. How much money did
    the town government have to pay?

    _____A. *In order to find the total cost, you must
             add the cost of running and maintain-
             ing the pool to the amount collected in
             user fees.*

    _____B. *You are given the total cost of running
             the pool and the part of the cost covered
             by user fees. In order to find the cost to
             the town government, you must
             subtract.*

5. Walter and Sebastian traveled from Chicago to
    Anchorage, arriving in Anchorage at 9 p.m. It is 4
    hours earlier in Anchorage than in Chicago. What
    was the time in Chicago when they arrived?

    _____A. *Anchorage's time is earlier. Therefore
             you must add four hours to the time in
             Anchorage to find Chicago's time.*

    _____B. *Since it is later in Anchorage, you must
             subtract to find Chicago's time.*

Answers on page 144.

SOLVING ADDITION AND SUBTRACTION WORD PROBLEMS
CONTAINING NO KEY WORDS

Sometimes an addition or subtraction word problem contains no key words. Restating the problem can be helpful in deciding when to add and when to subtract.

Example: Susan has already driven her car 2,700 miles since its last oil change. She still plans to drive 600 miles before changing the oil. How many miles does she plan to drive between oil changes?

Step 1:   *question:* How many miles does she plan to drive between oil changes?

Step 2:   *necessary information:* 2,700 miles, 600 miles

Step 3:   *decide what arithmetic to use:* You are given the number of miles Susan has already driven and the number of miles more that she plans to drive. You need to add these together to find the total number of miles between oil changes.

$$\begin{array}{r} 2,700 \\ +\ 600 \\ \hline 3,300 \end{array}$$

Step 4:   2,700 miles + 600 miles = **3,300 miles** between oil changes.

Step 5:   It makes sense that she will drive 3,300 miles between oil changes since you are looking for a number larger than the 2,700 miles that she has already driven.

EXERCISE 3:   Underline the necessary information. Select the correct restatement and then solve the problem.

1. After reading a 320-page novel, Danyel read a 205-page history book. How many pages did Danyel read?

   ＿＿A.   *Since you are looking for the total number of pages, you should add.*

   ＿＿B.   *To find the difference between the number of pages in the two books you should subtract.*

   ＿＿＿＿＿＿＿＿＿＿＿

2. After making 24 bowls, Claire made 16 plates. How many pieces did she make?

   ＿＿A.   *Since the number of pieces includes the number of bowls and plates, you must add them together.*

   ＿＿B.   *Since you are looking for a difference, you must subtract the number of plates from the number of bowls.*

   ＿＿＿＿＿＿＿＿＿＿＿

3. A plant has produced 48,624 microwave ovens so far this year. The company expects to produce 37,716 microwave ovens during the rest of the year. What is the projected production of ovens for the year?

_____ A. *To find the projected production for the year, you must subtract the number of microwave ovens to be produced from the number of ovens that have been produced so far.*

_____ B. *To find the projected production for the entire year, you must add the number of ovens already produced to the number of ovens that are expected to be produced.*

_____

4. Diane has a 50,000-mile warranty on her car. The car has gone 34,913 miles. As of today, how many miles will the car have left on its warranty?

_____ A. *In order to find the total number of miles that the car has left on warranty, you should add the number of miles she has driven to the number of miles that the warranty covers.*

_____ B. *Since Diane has driven on the warranty, you must subtract the miles she has already driven from the mileage that the warranty covers.*

_____

Answers on page 144.

USING PICTURES AND DIAGRAMS TO SOLVE WORD PROBLEMS

Another approach that people use to solve word problems is to get a "picture" of the problem. While some people can do this in their heads, many people find it very useful to draw a picture or diagram of the problem.

Drawing a picture or making a diagram is useful in working with quantities or amounts. The following examples illustrate ways that drawing diagrams and pictures can be useful.

Example 1:   Shirley now earns $130 a week. She will be getting a raise of $9 a week. What will her new salary be?

Step 1:   *question:* What will her new salary be?

Step 2:   *necessary information:* $130 a week, $9 a week

Step 3:   Draw a diagram and decide whether to add or subtract.

Since you are looking for her income after a raise, you should add.

Step 4:   Do the arithmetic.
$130 + $9 = $139

Step 5:   Make sure that your answer is sensible.

$$\begin{array}{r} 130 \\ + 9 \\ \hline 139 \end{array}$$

Example 2:   After a raise of $6 a week, Shirley now makes $154. What was her original salary?

Step 1:   *question:* What was her original salary?

Step 2:   *necessary information:* $6 a week, $154

Step 3:   Draw a diagram and decide whether to add or subtract.

Since you are looking for her income before a raise, you should subtract.

Step 4:   Do the arithmetic.
$154 − $6 = $148

Step 5:   Make sure that your answer is sensible.

$$\begin{array}{r} 154 \\ - 6 \\ \hline 148 \end{array}$$

In the first example above, the diagram helps to show that addition is necessary, while the second shows the need for subtraction. While these problems are fairly simple, practice in drawing diagrams can help you with more complicated problems.

Examples 3 and 4 below show how making a diagram can help you decide whether to add or subtract.

Example 3:   An oil-producing country charges $3 per barrel over the prevailing price for crude oil. A neighboring country charges $37, which is $2 under the prevailing price. How much does the first country charge?

Step 1:   *question:* How much does the first country charge?

Step 2:   *necessary information:* $3 per barrel, $37, $2

Step 3:   Draw a diagram and decide whether to add or subtract.

The diagram shows that you must perform two steps: 1) add 2 dollars to reach the prevailing price, and 2) add 3 more dollars to find the rate charged by the first country.

Step 4:   Do the arithmetic.
$37 + $3 + $2 = $42

Step 5:   Make sure that your answer is sensible.

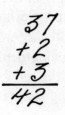

Example 4:   A recipe for 48 ounces of punch calls for 23 ounces of fruit juice and liquor. The rest is club soda. How much of the recipe is club soda?

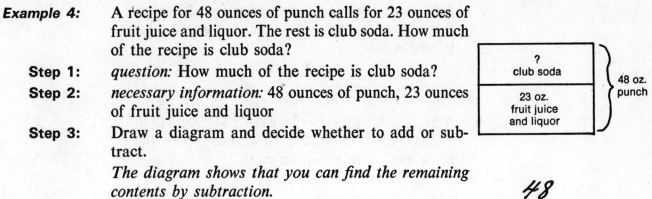

Step 1:   *question:* How much of the recipe is club soda?

Step 2:   *necessary information:* 48 ounces of punch, 23 ounces of fruit juice and liquor

Step 3:   Draw a diagram and decide whether to add or subtract.

The diagram shows that you can find the remaining contents by subtraction.

Step 4:   Do the arithmetic.

48 − 23 = 25

Step 5.   Make sure that your answer is sensible.

EXERCISE 4:   For each problem, make a drawing or a diagram and decide whether to add or subtract. Then solve the problem.

1.   If 3 more students are added to this class, we will have 31 students. How many students do we have now?

   _____

2.   Rafael Hernandez paid $39 less in taxes in 1981 than in 1982. He paid $483 in 1981. How much did he pay in 1982?

   _____

3.   San Francisco's time is one hour earlier than Denver's. New York's time is 2 hours later than Denver's. How many hours' difference is there between San Francisco and New York?

   _____

4.   12,000 gallons of water an hour flow through the dam spillway. The 41-year-old dam operator plans to decrease the flow by 3,500 gallons. What will be the new rate of water flow?

   _____

5. A $120 black and white television costs $359 less than a color television. How much does the color television cost?

_____

6. A black and white television costs $120 less than a $359 color television. How much does the black and white television cost?

_____

7. Between 6 p.m. and 11 p.m., the temperature decreased by 13 degrees to 61 degrees. What had the temperature been at 6 p.m.?

_____

8. At 6 p.m. the temperature was 61 degrees. Between 6 p.m. and 11 p.m., it decreased 13 degrees. What was the temperature at 11 p.m.?

_____

9. 1,412 people graduated from Lincoln High School in 1938. Today, 957 of these graduates are still living. How many of the graduates have died?

_____

10. Marion took out a loan for $6,000. She has paid back $3,800. How much does she still owe?

_____

11. During the Washington's Birthday Sale, Economy Motors sold 46 cars. During the rest of the month, 35 cars were sold. How many cars were sold by Economy Motors in February?

_____

12. A 2,600-pound truck can carry a 1,000-pound load. How much does the fully loaded truck weigh?

_____

13. This year, the average class size at South School has increased by 4 students to 29 students per class. What was the average class size last year?

_____

Answers on page 144.

USING NUMBER SENTENCES TO SOLVE WORD PROBLEMS

Addition and subtraction word problems can be solved by writing number sentences.

A number sentence restates a word problem first in words and then in numbers.

Example 1:   Lori went to school for 5 years in Levittown before moving to Plainview. She then went to school for 7 years in Plainview. For how many years did she go to school?

The following shows how to write a number sentence.

Write the information in the problem in words:

Levittown plus Plainview equals total years

Substitute numbers and mathematical symbols for the words:

5 years + 7 years = total years
Solve:

12 years = total years

$$\begin{array}{r} 5 \\ +7 \\ \hline 12 \end{array}$$

After some practice, it may not be necessary to write out the solution in words.

Example 2:   A play ran for two nights at a theater seating 270 people. 235 people saw the play the first night, and 261 people saw the play the second night. How many people saw the play during its two-night run?

Step 1:   *question:* How many people saw the play during its two-night run?

Step 2:   *necessary information:* 235 people, 261 people

Step 3:   *word sentence:*

first night + second night = total people

235 people + 261 people = total people

Step 4:   **496 people = total people**

$$\begin{array}{r} 235 \\ +261 \\ \hline 496 \end{array}$$

(The fact that the theater seats 270 people is not necessary information.)

Example 3: Gloria bought a $57 dress on sale for $19. How much did she save?

Step 1: *question:* How much did she save?

Step 2: *necessary information:* $57, $19

Step 3: *word sentence:*
original price − sale price = savings

Step 4: $57 − $19 = savings
$38 = savings

$$\begin{array}{r} 5\,7 \\ -\,1\,9 \\ \hline 3\,8 \end{array}$$

Hint: If you are looking for a total, write an addition sentence. If you are looking for a change or difference, write a subtraction sentence.

EXERCISE 5: Underline the necessary information. Write a word sentence and a number sentence. Then solve the problem and write the answer on the line below.

1. Ross needed a 13 cent stamp for a postcard. If he paid for the stamp with a quarter, how much change did he get?

    _____

2. Bruce drives 32 miles to work each day. When he arrived at work on Monday, he found that he had driven 51 miles that day. How many additional miles over his regular commuting distance had Bruce driven on Monday?

    _____

3. The box office sold 134 tickets to the play. The theater company needs to sell 172 tickets to break even. How many more tickets must they sell in order to break even?

    _____

4. Wendy decided to buy a $1,300 used car. She had saved $460. She got a loan for the rest. What was the amount of the loan?

    _____

5. Becci Bachman needs 150 names on her nominating petition to run for office. She collected 119 names on her first day of campaigning. How many more names does she have to collect?

   _____

6. After losing 47 pounds, Ann weighed 119. What was her original weight?

   _____

7. Lucy's monthly food stamp allotment was reduced by $13 to $68. How much was she getting in food stamps before the reduction?

   _____

8. A $365 refrigerator was marked down to $279. How much did Kathy save by buying the refrigerator on sale?

   _____

9. John had $213 withheld for federal income tax. In fact, he only owed $185. How much of a refund will he receive?

   _____

10. A car factory cut production by 3,500 cars to 8,200 cars a month. What had the monthly production been before the cutback?

    _____

11. Maria earned $8,682 dollars last year. She spent $7,991. How much did she save?

    _____

12. Mr. Crockett's cow Bertha produced 1,423 gallons of milk last year. His other cow, Calico, produced 1,289 gallons. How much milk did his cows produce last year?

_____

13. Memorial Stadium has 72,070 seats. 58,682 people had seats at the football game. How many seats were empty?

_____

14. In one garden bed, a gardener grew spinach, and when the spinach was harvested, he grew green beans. The spinach was harvested after 49 days. The green beans were harvested after 56 days. For how many days were vegetables growing in the garden bed?

_____

Answers on page 145.

CHAPTER 4:
Addition And Subtraction Word Problems: Decimals and Fractions

USING THE SUBSTITUTION METHOD

So far, you have solved whole number addition and subtraction word problems. Many students can do these word problems with ease, but they worry when they see word problems using large whole numbers, fractions, or decimals. If you already know how to add and subtract whole numbers, fractions, and decimals, you will be able to do any of these problems.

Read the following examples and think about their differences and similarities.

Example 1:   A cardboard manufacturer makes cardboard 4 mm thick. To save money, he plans to make cardboard 3 mm thick instead. How much thinner is the new cardboard?

Step 1:   *question:* How much thinner is the new cardboard?

Step 2:   *necessary information:* 4 mm, 3 mm

Step 3:   *decide what arithmetic to use:*

You are given the thickness of each piece of cardboard. Since you must find the difference between the two pieces, you should subtract.

$$\begin{array}{r} 4 \\ -3 \\ \hline 1 \end{array}$$

Step 4:   4 mm − 3mm = **1 mm**

> **Note:**   mm stands for millimeter. You should be able to do this type of problem even if you aren't already familiar with metric measurement.

Example 2:   A cardboard manufacturer makes cardboard 6.45 mm thick. To save money, he plans to make cardboard 5.5 mm thick instead. How much thinner is the new cardboard?

Step 1:   *question:* How much thinner is the new cardboard?

Step 2:   *necessary information:* 6.45 mm, 5.5 mm

Step 3:   *decide what arithmetic to use:*

You are given the thickness of each piece of cardboard. Since you must find the difference between the two pieces, you should subtract.

$$\begin{array}{r} 6.45 \\ -5.50 \\ \hline .95 \end{array}$$

Step 4:   6.45 mm − 5.50 mm = **.95 mm**

Example 3: A cardboard manufacturer makes cardboard $\frac{3}{8}$ in. thick. To save money, he plans to make cardboard $\frac{1}{3}$ in. thick instead. How much thinner is the new cardboard?

Step 1: *question:* How much thinner is the new cardboard?

Step 2: *necessary information:* $\frac{3}{8}$ in., $\frac{1}{3}$ in.

Step 3: *decide what arithmetic to use:*

You are given the thickness of each piece of cardboard. Since you must find the difference between the two pieces, you should subtract.

Step 4: $\frac{3}{8}$ in. $-$ $\frac{1}{3}$ in. $=$ $\frac{1}{24}$ **in.**

$$\begin{array}{r} \frac{3}{8} = \frac{9}{24} \\ -\frac{1}{3} = \frac{8}{24} \\ \hline \frac{1}{24} \end{array}$$

Note: Remember, in order to find the solution, you must change unlike fractions to fractions with the same common denominator.

What did you notice about the three example problems?

The wording of all three is exactly the same. Only the numbers and labels have been changed. All three problems are solved the same way, by subtracting.

Then why do Examples 2 and 3 seem harder than the first example?

It has to do with "math intuition," or the feel that a person has for numbers. You have a very clear idea of the correct answer to $4 - 3$. It is more difficult to picture $7,483,251 + 29,983$ or $6.45 - 5.5$. And for most of us, our intuition totally breaks down for $\frac{3}{8} - \frac{1}{3}$.

Changing only the numbers in a word problem does not change what must be done to solve the problem. By substituting small whole numbers in a problem, you can understand the problem and how to solve it.

Look at the following example:

Example 4: A floor is to be covered with a layer of $\frac{3}{4}$ in. fiberboard and $\frac{7}{16}$ in. plywood. By how much will the floor level be raised?

Fractions, especially those with different denominators, are especially hard to picture. You can make the problem easier to understand by substituting small whole numbers for the fractions. You can substitute any numbers, but try to use numbers under 10.

(These numbers do not have to look like the numbers they are replacing.)

In the problem above, try substituting 3 for $\frac{3}{4}$ and 2 for $\frac{7}{16}$.

The problem now looks like this:

A floor is to be covered by a layer of 3 in. fiberboard and 2 in. plywood. By how much will the floor level be raised?

You can now read this problem and know that you must add.

Once you make your decision about *how* to solve the problem, you can return the original numbers to the word problem and work out the solution. With the substituted numbers, you decided to *add* 3 and 2. Therefore, in the original, you must *add* $\frac{3}{4}$ and $\frac{7}{16}$.

$$\begin{array}{r} \frac{3}{4} = \frac{12}{16} \\ + \frac{7}{16} = \frac{7}{16} \\ \hline \frac{19}{16} = 1\frac{3}{16} \text{ inches} \end{array}$$

Remember: Choosing 3 and 2 was completely arbitrary. You could have used any small whole number.

EXERCISE 1:   At the end of the following set of word problems are six substitutions. Each of the substitutions will fit only one of the six word problems. In the answer space for each problem, write the letter of the correct substitution. (After each problem, you are told which numbers to substitute for that problem. To keep it simple, we are only using the numbers 4, 3, and 1 in the substitutions.)

1. A sweater that normally sells for $30.99 has been marked down by $10.99. What is the sale price of the sweater?
   Substitute $3 for $30.99 and $1 for $10.99.

   _____

2. Two round roasts weigh 3.46 and 4.17 pounds. How much heavier is the 4.17 pound roast?
   Substitute 3 for 3.46 and 4 for 4.17.

   _____

3. Robin bought a 3.28-pound steak and a 4.84-pound chicken. What was the weight of the meat she bought?
   Substitute 3 for 3.28 and 4 for 4.84.

   _____

4. Janice bought a dress for $31.99 and a skirt for $11.59. How much did she spend in all?
   Substitute $3 for $31.99 and $1 for $11.59.

   _____

5. Michael caught a $21\frac{1}{4}$ inch fish. His friend Paul caught a $23\frac{1}{16}$ inch fish. How much longer was Paul's fish?
   Substitute 1 for $21\frac{1}{4}$ and 3 for $23\frac{1}{16}$.

   _____

6. Two boards were placed end to end. The first board was $40\frac{7}{8}$ inches long. The second board was $32\frac{3}{4}$ inches long. What was the combined length of the two boards?
   Substitute 3 for $40\frac{7}{8}$ and 1 for $32\frac{3}{4}$.

   _____

A. 3 pounds + 4 pounds = 7 pounds
B. 4 pounds − 3 pounds = 1 pound
C. $3 − $1 = $2
D. $3 + $1 = $4
E. 3 inches + 1 inch = 4 inches
F. 3 inches − 1 inch = 2 inches

Answers on page 146.

USING APPROXIMATION TO ESTIMATE ANSWERS

When your car is in an accident and you take it to an auto body shop for repairs, you first receive an estimate for the cost of the repairs. This might not be the exact or final price, but it should be close.

When solving word problems, it is also important to have some idea of what the answer should be before you start doing the arithmetic. You can get an estimate of the answer by approximating the numbers in the problem.

An approximation is almost, but not quite, the exact number. For instance:

In the last election, the newspaper reported that Alderman Jones received 52% of the vote and his opponent received 48%. Actually, the Alderman received 52.1645% of the vote and his opponent received 47.8355%.

The newspaper did not report the exact percent of the vote; it rounded off the numbers to the nearest whole percent. Rounded-off numbers are one type of estimate.

Estimating the numbers and doing quick arithmetic in your head is a good way to check your work.

EXERCISE 2: Read the following statements. Then write an approximation of each of the numbers in the space provided. Each problem tells you to what place you should round off.

1. 10,043 people died from handguns last year.
   To the nearest thousand

   _____

2. 1,013,308 birds were counted this winter.
   To the nearest million

   _____

3. 44,812 were at the baseball game at Memorial Stadium.
To the nearest thousand

_____

4. The turkey weighed 22.15 pounds.
To the nearest pound

_____

5. Karen is 5 feet $4\frac{7}{8}$ inches tall.
To the nearest inch

_____

Answers on page 146.

EXERCISE 3:   Match each word problem with an estimated solution. The numbers in the solutions have been rounded off. Write the letter of the correct estimated solution in the answer space.

1. During the last weekend in July, 35,142 fans saw the baseball game on Saturday. 36,994 fans saw the game on Sunday. What was the total attendance for the weekend?

_____

2. Nationwide, Grand Discount Stores sold 37,238 fans in April and 34,982 fans in May. How many more fans were sold in April?

_____

3. The original estimate for the cost of a nuclear power plant was .984 billion dollars. The final cost was 4.16 billion dollars. How much did the price increase from the original estimate?

_____

4. The state budget is 3.92 billion dollars. It is expected to increase 1.2 billion dollars over the next five years. How much is the budget expected to be five years from now?

_____

5. By expressway, it is $7\frac{1}{4}$ miles to the beach. By back roads, it is $8\frac{9}{10}$ miles. How much shorter is the trip when driving by expressway?

_____

6. Pat is a long distance runner. He ran $6\frac{9}{10}$ miles on Saturday and $9\frac{1}{8}$ miles on Sunday. How many miles in all did he run during the weekend?

_____

A. 9 miles − 7 miles = 2 miles
B. 9 miles + 7 miles = 16 miles
C. 4 billion dollars − 1 billion dollars = 3 billion dollars
D. 4 billion dollars + 1 billion dollars = 5 billion dollars
E. 37,000 fans − 35,000 fans = 2,000 fans
F. 37,000 fans + 35,000 fans = 72,000 fans

Answers on page 146.

DECIMAL ADDITION AND SUBTRACTION WORD PROBLEMS: RESTATING THE PROBLEM

Restating the problem is one method that will work as well with solving decimal problems as with whole number problems. Don't worry about the decimal points until after you have decided to add or subtract. Then, remember to line up the decimal points before doing the arithmetic.

Example: A pair of pants was on sale for $8.99. A shirt was on sale for $6.49. Alan decided to buy both. How much did he spend?

Step 1:   *question:* How much did he spend?

Step 2:   *necessary information:* $8.99, $6.49

Step 3:   *restatement:* Since Alan is buying both items, you must add to find the total amount he spent.

Step 4: $8.99 + $6.49 = **$15.48**

Step 5:   An approximation for $8.99 is $9 and for $6.49 is $6.50.

$9 + $6.50 = $15.50.

Therefore, your answer should be close to $15.50. Making an approximation is a good method of checking your answer and making sure it is sensible.

$$\begin{array}{r} 8.99 \\ + 6.49 \\ \hline 15.48 \end{array}$$

EXERCISE 4:   Circle the letter of the correct restatement, and then solve the problem. Use approximation to make sure your answer is sensible.

1. Using his odometer, George discovered that one route to work was 6.3 miles long and the other was 7.1 miles. How much shorter was the first way?

    A. *Since you are given the two distances to work, add to find out how much shorter the first way was.*

    B. *To find how much shorter the first way was, subtract to find the difference.*

    _____

2. Max had to put gasoline in his 8-year-old car twice last week. The first time he put in 9.4 gallons. The second time he put in 14.7 gallons. How much gasoline did he put in his car last week?

    A. *To find the total amount of gasoline he put in his car, you must add.*

    B. *Since you are given the two amounts of gasoline, you must subtract to find the difference.*

    _____

3. The first fish fillet weighed 1.42 pounds. The second fillet weighed .98 pound. Alice decided to buy both fillets. What was the weight of the fish she bought?

    A. *To find the total weight of the two fish, you must add.*

    B. *Since you are given the weight of the two fish, you must subtract to find the difference between their weights.*

    _____

4. At the Reckless Speedway, Bobby was clocked at 198.7 mph while Mario was clocked at 200.15 mph. How much faster did Mario drive than Bobby?

A. *You must add the two speeds to find how much faster Mario drove.*

B. *Since Mario drove faster, subtract Bobby's speed from his to find out the difference between speeds.*

_____

5. Last year, the unemployment rate was 7.9%. This year, it has increased to 9.1%. By how much did unemployment rise?

A. *In order to find how much unemployment rose, you must add the two unemployment rates.*

B. *In order to find the rise in unemployment, you must subtract last year's rate from this year's rate.*

_____

6. A side of beef weighs 12.6 pounds. Ann bought 3.82 pounds from the side. What was the weight of the side of beef after Ann's purchase?

A. *To find the new weight of the side of beef, you must subtract the amount removed from the original weight.*

B. *To find the new weight of the side of beef, you must add the weights of the two pieces of meat.*

_____

7. Two metal bars were welded together. One bar was .7 inch thick. The other was .375 inch thick. How thick is the welded bar?

A. *To find the size of the welded bar, you must subtract the size of the smaller bar from the size of the larger bar.*

B. *Since the bars are to be welded together, you must add the size of the two bars to find the thickness of the new bar.*

_____

Answers on page 146.

DECIMAL ADDITION AND SUBTRACTION PROBLEMS:
DRAWINGS AND DIAGRAMS

Diagrams and drawings can help you solve decimal addition or subtraction word problems.

Example: A metal bearing was .24 cm thick. The machinist ground it down until it was .065 cm thinner. How thick was the metal bearing after it had been ground down?

--.24 cm thick
---.065 cm ground down
-----new thickness

Step 1: *question:* How thick was the metal bearing after it had been ground down?

Step 2: *necessary information:* .24 cm, .065 cm

Step 3: *make a drawing:*

To find the size of the bearing after it was ground down, you must subtract.

Step 4: Do the arithmetic. Be sure to line up the decimal points. If you add a zero, you can see that .24 (.240) is larger than .065.

.240 cm − .065 cm = **.175 cm**

$$\begin{array}{r} .240 \\ -.065 \\ \hline .175 \end{array}$$

Remember: When subtracting decimals, first line up the decimal points. Then fill any blank spaces to the right of the point with zeros. This should help you borrow correctly.

EXERCISE 5: Make a drawing or a diagram and then solve the problem. (Each person's drawing may be different. What is important is that the diagram makes sense to you.)

1. Meatball subs used to cost $1.60 at Mike's, but he just raised the price $.25. How much do meatball subs cost now?

   _____

2. Tara's prescription for .55 gram of antibiotic was not strong enough. Her doctor gave her a new prescription for .7 gram of antibiotic. How much stronger was the new prescription?

   _____

3. Mike Johnson was hitting .342 before he went into a batting slump. By the end of his slump, his average had dropped .083. What was his batting average at the end of his slump?

_____

4. Joyce's income of $113.50 had $26.13 taken out for deductions. How much was her take-home pay?

_____

5. A wooden peg is 1.6 inches wide and 3.2 inches long. It can be squeezed into an opening .05 inch smaller than the width of the peg. What is the width of the opening?

_____

6. By midweek, Wendy had spent $46.65. At the end of the week, she had spent $23.35 more. How much had Wendy spent that week?

_____

7. The gap of a spark plug should be .08 inch. The plug would still work if the gap is off by as much as .015 inch. What is the largest gap that would still work?

_____

8. The King Coal Company mined 126.4 tons of coal. 18.64 tons of coal were unusable because of high sulfur content. How many tons of coal were usable?

_____

Answers on page 146.

DECIMAL ADDITION AND SUBTRACTION WORD PROBLEMS:
WRITING NUMBER SENTENCES

Number sentences can help you solve decimal addition and subtraction word problems. Remember, when solving decimal word problems, it is important to write the number sentence first. Then you should add or subtract, lining up the decimal points. Finally, you should check to see if your answer is sensible.

Example 1: Meryl bought $16.27 worth of groceries and paid with a $20 bill. How much change did she receive?

Step 1: *question:* How much change did she receive?

Step 2: *necessary information:* $16.27, $20 bill

Step 3: *word sentence:*
amount paid − price of groceries = change

Step 4: *number sentence:*
$20 − $16.27 = change
$3.73 = change

$$\begin{array}{r} 20.00 \\ -16.27 \\ \hline 3.73 \end{array}$$

Example 2: On sale, a pair of pants costs $12.49. They had been discounted $4.49 from the original price. What had the original price been?

Step 1: *question:* What had the original price been?

Step 2: *necessary information:* $4.49, $12.49

Step 3: sale price + discount = original price

Step 4: $12.49 + $4.49 = original price
$16.98 = original price

$$\begin{array}{r} 12.49 \\ +4.49 \\ \hline 16.98 \end{array}$$

EXERCISE 6: Underline the necessary information. Write a word sentence and a number sentence. Then solve the problem.

1. The Sticky Candy Company decided to reduce the size of their chocolate candy bar by .6 ounce to 2.4 ounces. How much did their chocolate bar weigh before the change?

   _____

2. Julie's lunch cost $2.38. If she paid with a $10.00 bill, how much change did she get?

   _____

3. Bernice bought one chicken that weighed 3.94 pounds and one that weighed 4.68 pounds. She also bought a 1.32 pound steak. How much chicken did she buy?

    _____

4. When Mark left Boston, the odometer of his car read 23,172.3 miles. When he arrived in New York, it read 23,391.4 miles. How long was his trip?

    _____

5. To get to her mother's house, Connie has to take the bus and the subway. The bus costs $.40 and the subway costs $.65. How much will it cost altogether for Connie to take a one-way trip to her mother's?

    _____

6. Judy spent $341.98 for a new washing machine in Massachusetts. If she had bought the same machine in New Hampshire, she would have paid $335.26 since it does not have a sales tax. How much less would she have paid in New Hampshire?

    _____

7. When he ran the 200 meter race, Marcus ran the first 100 meters in 14.36 seconds and the second 100 meters in 13.9 seconds. What was his total time for the race?

    _____

Answers on page 147.

FRACTION ADDITION AND SUBTRACTION WORD PROBLEMS:
RESTATING THE PROBLEM

Before solving these fraction problems, you might want to use either substitution or approximation to help you decide what arithmetic to use. In this section, you will restate the problem in order to decide whether to add or subtract.

Example: Tanya grew $2\frac{3}{4}$ inches last year. If she was $42\frac{1}{2}$ inches tall a year ago, how tall is she now?

Step 1:   *question:* How tall is she now?

Step 2:   *necessary information:* $2\frac{3}{4}$ inches, $42\frac{1}{2}$ inches

Step 3:   *restatement:* Since you know Tanya's old height, and you know that she grew, you must add to find her new height.

Step 4: $2\frac{3}{4}$ inches + $42\frac{1}{2}$ inches = height now

$2\frac{3}{4} + 42\frac{2}{4} = 44\frac{5}{4}$ inches = **$45\frac{1}{4}$ inches now**

$$\begin{array}{r} 2\frac{3}{4} = 2\frac{3}{4} \\ +42\frac{1}{2} = 42\frac{2}{4} \\ \hline 44\frac{5}{4} = 45\frac{1}{4} \end{array}$$

Remember: Find a common denominator whenever you add or subtract fractions.

EXERCISE 7:   Each problem is followed by two restatements and approximations; write either A or B on the first line. Then, solve the problem and write the exact solution on the second line.

1.   A carpenter needed one piece of molding $28\frac{1}{2}$ inches long, and a second piece $31\frac{1}{4}$ inches long. How much molding did he need?

   A.   *To find out how much molding is needed, you must subtract.*
   31 inches − 29 inches = 2 inches

   B.   *To find the total amount of molding needed, you must add.*
   29 inches + 31 inches = 60 inches

   _____

   _____

2.   Vera combined $1\frac{2}{3}$ cups of flour and $1\frac{1}{3}$ cups of butter in a 2-quart mixing bowl. How many cups of the mixture did Vera have?

   A.   *Since Vera is combining the flour and butter, the amount of the mixture can be found by adding.*
   2 cups + 1 cup = 3 cups

B. *Since you are given the amount of flour
and the amount of butter, you must
subtract to find the amount of the
mixture.*

2 cups − 1 cup = 1 cup

———————

————————————————

3. Tara weighs $71\frac{1}{4}$ pounds. Her younger sister,
Erinne weighs $62\frac{1}{2}$ pounds. How much heavier
is Tara than Erinne?

A. *Since you are comparing two weights, you
must subtract to find the difference.*

71 pounds − 63 pounds = 8 pounds

B. *Since you are finding Tara's total weight,
you must add the given weights.*

71 pounds + 63 pounds = 134 pounds.

———————

————————————————

4. Mira was $18\frac{3}{4}$ inches tall at birth. Six months
later, she was $23\frac{1}{4}$ inches tall. How much taller
was Mira after six months than at birth?

A. *To find how much taller Mira is, you must
add the given heights.*

19 inches + 23 inches = 42 inches

B. *To find how much taller Mira is, you must
subtract her birth height from her height at
six months.*

23 inches − 19 inches = 4 inches

———————

————————————————

Answers on page 147.

FRACTION ADDITION AND SUBTRACTION WORD PROBLEMS: DIAGRAMS AND PICTURES

Making diagrams and pictures can also help you solve fraction addition or subtraction word problems. To help you with your solution, use either the approximation or the substitution method.

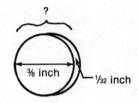

Example: Using a $\frac{3}{8}$-inch drill bit, Judy drilled a hole that was slightly too small. She used the next size drill bit, one that was $\frac{1}{32}$ inch larger, to enlarge the hole. What was the size of the new drill bit?

Step 1:   *question:* What was the size of the new drill bit?

Step 2:   *necessary information:* $\frac{3}{8}$ inch, $\frac{1}{32}$ inch.

Step 3:   draw a picture
decide what arithmetic to use

Step 4:   Since you are looking for the next larger size, you must add.

$\frac{3}{8}$ inch + $\frac{1}{32}$ inch = $\frac{12}{32}$ inch + $\frac{1}{32}$ inch=

$\frac{13}{32}$ inch

$$\frac{3}{8} = \frac{12}{32}$$
$$+ \frac{1}{32} = \frac{1}{32}$$
$$\overline{\frac{13}{32}}$$

EXERCISE 8:   Make a drawing or diagram and then solve the problems below.

1. What is called a "2-by-4" (a 2 inch by 4 inch board) is really not 4 inches high. It is actually $\frac{5}{8}$ inch smaller. What is the real height of the board?

    _____

2. Pat is at the hospital for a total of $8\frac{1}{2}$ hours a day. If during each day he has $1\frac{3}{4}$ hours for breaks, how long does he work each day?

    _____

3. Hope worked $6\frac{1}{2}$ hours and took an additional $\frac{3}{4}$ hour for lunch. What was the total amount of time that Hope spent at work and lunch?

    _____

4. A 2 inch by 4 inch board is really not 2 inches wide. It is $\frac{1}{2}$ inch narrower. What is the real width of the board?

_____

5. A recipe called for $2\frac{1}{2}$ cups of flour. George only had $1\frac{2}{3}$ cups. How much flour did he have to borrow from his neighbor?

_____

Answers on page 147.

FRACTION ADDITION AND SUBTRACTION WORD PROBLEMS: USING NUMBER SENTENCES

Number sentences can also help you solve fraction addition or subtraction word problems.

Example: David planned to make a 3-inch-thick insulated roof. The roof will be made with a layer of thermal board on top of $\frac{5}{8}$-inch plywood. How thick can the thermal board be?

Step 1:   *question:* How thick can the thermal board be?
Step 2:   *necessary information:* 3 inches, $\frac{5}{8}$ inch
Step 3:   *word sentence:*
                thickness of roof − plywood = thermal board
Step 4:   3 inches − $\frac{5}{8}$ inch = thermal board
                $2\frac{3}{8}$ inches = thermal board

$$3 = 2\frac{8}{8}$$
$$-\frac{5}{8} = -\frac{5}{8}$$
$$\overline{ = 2\frac{3}{8}}$$

EXERCISE 9:   Write a word sentence and a number sentence. Then solve the word problems below.

1. Beverly filled a 3-quart punch bowl with punch. If she used $1\frac{1}{4}$ quarts of rum, how many quarts of other ingredients did she use?

_____

2. Amy bought a skirt that was $34\frac{1}{2}$ inches long. If she shortened it to $32\frac{3}{4}$ inches, how much did she take off?

_____

3. After 3 weeks in the store, a bolt of cloth that had originally been 20 yards long was $6\frac{1}{2}$ yards long. Then, $3\frac{2}{3}$ more yards of the cloth were sold. How much cloth was left?

_____

4. A meatball recipe called for $1\frac{1}{2}$ pounds of beef and $\frac{3}{4}$ pound of pork. How much meat was needed in the recipe?

_____

5. Last winter, Fred used $\frac{1}{8}$ cord of wood one week and $\frac{1}{12}$ cord of wood the next to heat his house. How much wood did he use during the two weeks?

_____

6. Linda bought $62\frac{1}{2}$ inches of cloth to make drapes. She used $\frac{3}{4}$ inch for the hem. How long was the drape?

_____

Answers on page 148.

REVIEW: SOLVING ADDITION AND SUBTRACTION
WORD PROBLEMS

The following exercise is a review of the first four chapters of this book.

EXERCISE 10: Solve each problem and circle the letter of the correct answer.

1. The Hammerhead Nail Company produces 55,572 nails and 4,186 screws a day. On Monday, 1,263 nails were no good. How many good nails were made on Monday?

   a. *56,835 nails*
   b. *54,309 nails*
   c. *59,758 nails*
   d. *51,386 nails*
   e. *58,495 nails*

2. Ana Marie had $75.62 in her wallet. How much
    money did she have after spending $38.56?

    a. *$114.18*
    b. *$37.06*
    c. *$1.98*
    d. *$114.06*
    e. *none of the above*

3. Ron got 16.2 miles per gallon using regular
    gasoline. After switching to gasohol, he got 19.1
    miles per gallon. How much did his mileage im-
    prove?

    a. *4.13 miles*
    b. *29 miles*
    c. *41.3 miles per gallon*
    d. *2.9 miles per gallon*
    e. *1.15 miles per gallon*

4. When Kathy bought her car, she paid $800 down
    and had $640 left in her savings account. She
    then paid $2,400 over the next two years to finish
    paying for the car. How much did the car cost
    her?

    a. *$3,840*
    b. *$1,600*
    c. *$300*
    d. *$3,200*
    e. *$2,560*

5. Before cooking, a hamburger weighed $\frac{1}{4}$ pound.
    After cooking, it weighed $\frac{3}{16}$ pound. The rest of
    the hamburger was fat that burned off during
    cooking. How much fat burned off during
    cooking?

    a. $\frac{4}{20}$ *pound*
    b. $\frac{1}{6}$ *pound*
    c. $\frac{1}{16}$ *pound*
    d. $\frac{7}{16}$ *pound*
    e. *none of the above*

6. Brand X contains .47 gram of pain reliever per 1.5 gram tablet. Brand Y contains .6 gram of pain reliever. How much more pain reliever does Brand Y have than Brand X?

    a. .53 gram
    b. .41 gram
    c. .13 gram
    d. .27 gram
    e. 2.57 grams

7. A public television station has already raised $391,445 and must raise $528,555 more to stay in business. What was the target amount for the station's fundraising drive?

    a. $920,000
    b. $137,110
    c. $127,110
    d. $237,110
    e. none of the above

8. Joe bought a $26\frac{3}{4}$-inch windowshade. When he got home, he found out that it was $2\frac{3}{8}$ inches too narrow. What size windowshade does he need?

    a. $24\frac{3}{8}$ inches
    b. $29\frac{1}{8}$ inches
    c. $28\frac{1}{2}$ inches
    d. 24 inches
    e. none of the above

9. Last winter, Mrs. George used $\frac{5}{8}$ cord of wood in February, and $\frac{1}{12}$ cord of wood in March to heat her house. How much wood did she use?

    a. $\frac{3}{10}$ cord
    b. $\frac{13}{24}$ cord
    c. $\frac{1}{2}$ cord
    d. $\frac{3}{4}$ cord
    e. none of the above

10. A gallon of economy paint contained 3.4 tubes of pigment per gallon. The high quality paint contained 5.15 tubes of pigment per gallon. What was the difference between the amount of pigment used for each paint?

    a. 4.81 tubes
    b. 5.49 tubes
    c. 8.55 tubes
    d. 2.35 tubes
    e. none of the above

11. The United States leased 420,000 acres of the continental shelf at one time, 96,500 acres after that, and 123,460 acres much later. How much larger was the first leasing than the second?

    a. *516,500 acres*
    b. *200,040 acres*
    c. *323,500 acres*
    d. *639,960 acres*
    e. *296,540 acres*

12. The United States leased 420,000 acres of continental shelf in one sale, 96,500 acres in a second sale, and 123,460 acres in a third sale. What was the total amount of acres leased?

    a. *516,500 acres*
    b. *200,040 acres*
    c. *323,500 acres*
    d. *639,960 acres*
    e. *296,540 acres*

13. A radioactive tracer lost $\frac{1}{2}$ of its radioactivity in an hour. Three hours later it had lost another $\frac{7}{16}$ of its radioactivity. What was the total loss in radioactivity for the entire time?

    a. $\frac{7}{32}$ *of its radioactivity*
    b. $\frac{15}{16}$ *of its radioactivity*
    c. $\frac{4}{9}$ *of its radioactivity*
    d. $\frac{1}{16}$ *of its radioactivity*
    e. *none of the above*

14. To get pink paint, an artist mixed $\frac{3}{4}$ ounce of red paint with $\frac{1}{3}$ ounce of white paint. How much pink paint did she make?

    a. *2 ounces*
    b. $\frac{5}{12}$ *ounce*
    c. $1\frac{1}{12}$ *ounces*
    d. $\frac{4}{7}$ *ounce*
    e. *none of the above*

15. A gypsy moth grew .03 gram from 2.77 grams. How much did the gypsy moth weigh?

    a. *2.08 grams*
    b. *2.74 grams*
    c. *3.1 grams*
    d. *2.8 grams*
    e. *none of the above*

Answers on page 148.

CHAPTER 5:
Multiplication and Division Word Problems: Whole Numbers

In arithmetic, there are four basic operations: addition, subtraction, multiplication, and division. In Chapters 2 through 4, you looked at two operations: addition and subtraction. In Chapters 5 through 7, you will focus on the other two operations: multiplication and division.

As you have seen, subtraction can be thought of as the opposite of addition. In the same way, division can be thought of as the opposite of multiplication. This concept is useful in deciding whether a problem is a multiplication or a division problem.

IDENTIFYING MULTIPLICATION KEY WORDS

In Chapter 2, you looked at addition and subtraction key words. There are also multiplication key words.

Example 1:   Diane always bets $2 on a race. Last night she bet 8 times. How much money did she bet?

multiplication key word: times

Example 2:   It cost Fernando $9 per day to rent a car. He rented a car for 4 days. How much did he pay to rent the car?

multiplication key word: per

Remember: per means "for each."

Multiplication can also be considered repeated addition. Therefore, it is possible for an addition key word to also be a multiplication key word. "Total" is a word that can indicate either addition or multiplication.

EXERCISE 1:   In the following problems, circle the multiplication key words. DO NOT SOLVE!!

1. Miguel pays his landlord $170 rent 12 times a year. How much rent does he pay in a year?

2. During the 9 months that she stayed in her apartment, Isabelle paid $23 per month for electricity. How much did she pay for electricity during the time she stayed in her apartment?

3. At the stable, one horse eats 3 pounds of hay a day. What is the total amount of hay needed to feed 26 horses?

4. When her children were young, Alzette had a part time job for 18 hours a week. She now works twice as many hours as she did then. How many hours a week does she work now?

Answers on page 149.

SOLVING MULTIPLICATION WORD PROBLEMS
WITH KEY WORDS

Look at the following examples of multiplication key words:

Example 1: Shirley cleans the kitchen sink 3 times a week. How many times does she clean the sink in 4 weeks?

Step 1: *question:* How many times does she clean the sink?

Step 2: *necessary information:* 3 times a week, 4 weeks

Step 3: *decide what arithmetic to use:*
multiplication key word: times

Step 4: 3 times a week × 4 weeks = **12 times**

$$\begin{array}{r} 3 \\ \times\, 4 \\ \hline 12 \end{array}$$

Example 2: During the Depression, eggs cost 14 cents per dozen. How much did 5 dozen eggs cost?

Step 1: *question:* How much did 5 dozen eggs cost?

Step 2: *necessary information:* 14 cents per dozen, 5 dozen

Step 3: *decide what arithmetic to use:*
multiplication key word: per

Step 4: $.14 per dozen × 5 = **$.70**

$$\begin{array}{r} .14 \\ \times\, 5 \\ \hline .70 \end{array}$$

EXERCISE 2: In the problems below, underline the necessary information and circle the multiplication key words. Then solve the problem.

1. Artificially-flavored vanilla ice cream costs 42 cents a pint. All-natural vanilla ice cream costs twice as much. How much does the all-natural ice cream cost?

_____

Remember: Sometimes, numbers are written out as words.

2. Alan needs to buy 4 sets of guitar strings. There are 6 strings per set. How many strings will he buy?

_____

3. Honest Furniture Company's advertisement plays
    on the radio five times a day and appears in twelve
    newspapers. How many times does their ad play
    on radio in a week?

    _____

4. A regular-size soda is 8 ounces. Paula's Diner sold
    473 regular-size sodas in one day. What was the
    total amount of soda that the diner sold?

    _____

5. The We Fix-it Repair Company charges $47 per
    hour to repair typewriters. The We Fix-it
    repairman worked for 3 hours repairing
    typewriters at the Best Business School. How
    much did the business school pay to get its
    typewriters repaired?

    _____

Answers on page 149.

IDENTIFYING DIVISION KEY WORDS

As you should suspect by now, there are also division key words.

Example 1:   Harvey and Nancy split the cost of a $42 keg of beer.
                How much did each of them pay?

                division key word: split

                Remember: Any word indicating that something is
                               cut up is a division key word.

Example 2:   The police found 1,000 grams of heroin that had been
                divided evenly into 40 bags. How much heroin was in
                each bag?

                division key words: divided evenly, each

                "Each" is considered a division key word, since it
                indicates that you are given many things and are
                looking for one.

EXERCISE 3:   Circle the division key words. DO NOT SOLVE!

1. Carlos, Dan and Juan split the driving evenly when they drove 2,436 miles from Chicago to Los Angeles. How much did each of them drive?

2. A bakery produced 6,300 chocolate chip cookies in a day. The cookies were packed in boxes with 36 cookies in each box. How many boxes were used each day?

3. 3 salesmen sold $2,250 worth of power tools. On the average, how much did each of them sell?

4. It cost $36 to rent the gym for the basketball game. If the 12 players shared the cost evenly, how much did each of them pay?

Answers on page 149.

SOLVING DIVISION WORD PROBLEMS WITH KEY WORDS

Knowing the division key words can help you solve division word problems.

Example 1:   Union dues of $104 a year can be split up into 52 weekly payments. How much is a weekly payment?

Step 1:   *question:* How much is a weekly payment?

Step 2:   *necessary information:* $104 a year, 52 weekly payments

Step 3:   *division key word:* split up

Step 4: $104 ÷ 52 weekly payments = **$2**

$$52\overline{)104}\ \ ^{2}$$

Example 2:   A 10-pound cheese was cut into 5 equal pieces. How much did each piece weigh?

Step 1:   *question:* How much did each piece weigh?

Step 2:   *necessary information:* 10 pounds, 5 equal pieces

Step 3:   *division key words:* cut, equal pieces, each

Step 4:   10 pounds ÷ 5 equal payments = **2 pounds**

$$5\overline{)10}\ \ ^{2}$$

Example 3:   A 48-minute basketball game is divided into 4 equal periods. How long is each period?

Step 1:   *question:* How long is each period?

Step 2:   *necessary information:* 48-minute, 4 equal periods

Step 3:   *division key words:* divided, equal periods, each

Step 4:   48 minutes ÷ 4 periods = **12 minutes**

$$4\overline{)48}\ \ ^{12}$$

EXERCISE 4:   For the problems below, underline the necessary information and circle the division key words. Then solve the word problem.

1. A 12-oz. chocolate bar was shared equally by 4 children. How much chocolate did each child receive?

     _____

2. A 60-minute hockey game is divided into 3 equal periods. How long is each period?

     _____

3. A washing machine that costs $319 when new costs $156 used and can be paid for in 12 monthly payments. How much is each payment on the used washer?

     _____

4. A pack of 24 cigarettes costs 96 cents. How much does each cigarette cost?

     _____

5. Raffle tickets cost $3 each. If the prizes are worth $4,629, how many tickets must be sold for the raffle to break even?

     _____

6. A taxi fleet of 14 taxis burned 336 gallons of gasoline in one day. On the average, how much gasoline did each taxi burn?

     _____

Answers on page 149.

MULTIPLICATION AND DIVISION KEY WORD LISTS

As with addition and subtraction, we can compile lists of multiplication and division key words.

Multiplication Key Words

multiplied
times
total
of
per
as much
twice
by
area
volume

Generally, in multiplication word problems, you are given one of something and asked to find many. You can also think of these problems as multiplying together two parts to get a total.

Division Key Words

divided (evenly)
split
each
cut
equal pieces
average
every
out of
ratio
shared

Generally, in division word problems, you are given many things and asked to find one. You can also think of these problems as dividing a total by a part to get the other part.

Remember: Key words are only a clue for solving a problem. Any key word can also appear in word problems needing the opposite operation in order to be solved.

SOLVING MULTIPLICATION AND DIVISION WORD PROBLEMS WITH KEY WORDS

EXERCISE 5: In the next exercise, some of the word problems have multiplication key words and some have division key words. In each problem, circle the key words. On the first answer line, identify the circled word as a multiplication or division key word. Then solve the problem and fill in the answer on the second answer line.

1. An eight-slice pizza is to be divided evenly among four people. How many pieces will each person get?

   _____

   _____

2. An oil well made a profit of $90,000 last year. How much money will each of the five investors receive if all of the profits are split evenly among them?

   _____

   _____

3. A gas station owner charges $12 per oil change. In one day he did 15 oil changes. What was the total amount of money he received for oil changes?

   _____

   _____

4. In the discount store, a dress cost $27. In an expensive downtown store, the same dress cost twice as much. How much did the dress cost at the expensive store?

   _____

   _____

5. In order to earn a high school equivalency certificate, a student in Illinois must score 225 points on five tests but no less than 35 points on each test. What is the average score on each test that a student needs to get the certificate?

   _____

   _____

6. Last year in Boston, it rained 48 inches. On the average, how much did it rain during each of the 12 months?

_____

_____

7. A 3,500-gram wedding cake is to be cut into 175 equal pieces. How much will each piece weigh?

_____

_____

Answers on page 150.

DECIDING WHEN TO MULTIPLY AND WHEN TO DIVIDE

Word problems are rarely so simple that you can automatically solve them just by finding key words. You must develop your comprehension of the meaning of word problems. Key words are an aid to that understanding.

In earlier chapters, you learned that the same key word that helped you decide to add in one problem might also appear in a subtraction problem. The same is true with multiplication and division key words.

But Don't Despair!

Learning what the key words mean is the first step to understanding word problems.

In the examples that follow, you are given two numbers and are asked to find a third. In each example, you must decide whether to multiply or divide.

The question will ask you to find a total amount or it will give you a total amount and ask you to find a part.

- When you are given the parts and asked to find the total, you must multiply.
- When you are given the total and a part and you are asked to find a missing part, you must divide.

To get a better idea of this and of what is meant by "part" and "total," read the two examples below.

Example 1:   Each of the city's 24 snowplows can plow 94 miles of road a day. How many miles of road can be covered by the city plows in one day?

Example 2:   A city has 24 snowplows to plow its 2,256 miles of road. How many miles of road must each snowplow cover in order that all the city's roads are plowed?

The two examples on the previous page are really discussing the same situation. In the first example, the number of plows and miles for each plow are given; you are asked to find the total number of miles that can be covered, and you must multiply. In the second example, the total number of miles are given as well as the number of plows to be used. In this case, you are looking for a missing part (the miles for each plow) and must divide.

As you saw in earlier chapters, drawing diagrams is a good way to better understand a word problem. A simple diagram can be used to help you figure out whether you are looking for a total or a part.

Look at the diagram below. It can help you solve Examples 1 and 2.

Example 1:   Each of the city's 24 snowplows can plow 94 miles of road a day. If all snowplows are running, how many miles of road can be plowed by the city plows in one day?

Step 1:   *the question:* How many miles of road can be plowed?

Step 2:   *necessary information:* 24 snowplows, 94 miles of road.

Step 3:   *decide what arithmetic to do:* Use the following method to draw a diagram.
Draw two boxes and label them "part" and "part."
Put another box above them and label it "total."
Fill in the boxes with information from the problem. Use only the information that is needed to solve the problem.
Put 24 in the first "part" box since that is the number of snowplows. Put 94 in the other "part" box since that is the number of miles each snowplow can plow.
The box that is empty represents the amount that you are looking for, the total number of miles of road.

Step 4:   Since the box representing the total is empty, you should multiply.

snowplows × miles per snowplow = total miles

24 snowplows × 94 miles = **2,256 miles**

$$\begin{array}{r} 94 \\ \times 24 \\ \hline 2{,}256 \end{array}$$

Example 2:   A city has 24 snowplows to plow 2,256 miles of road. How many miles of road must each snowplow plow in order to plow all the city's roads?

Step 1:   *question:* How many miles of road must each snowplow plow?

Step 2:   *necessary information:* 24 snowplows, 2,256 miles of road

Step 3:   Draw and label the boxes.

Fill in the information needed to solve the problem.

Put 24 in the first "part" box since that is the number of snowplows. Put 2,256 in the "total" box since that has been given as the total number of miles.

The box that is empty represents the amount that you are looking for.

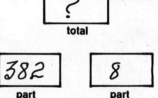

Step 4:   Since the total has been given you should divide to find the missing part.

total miles ÷ snowplows = miles per snowplow

2,256 miles ÷ 24 snowplows = **94 miles**

$$24\overline{)2{,}256}$$ with quotient 94

Example 3:   A cafeteria serves 382 people a day with 8-ounce portions of soup. How many ounces of soup must it make in one day?

Step 1:   *question:* How much soup must it make in one day?

Step 2:   *necessary information:* 382 people, 8-ounce portion of soup

Step 3:   Draw and label the boxes.

Fill in the information needed to solve the problem.

Put 382 in the first "part" box since that is the number of people. Put 8 in the other "part" box since that is the size of each portion.

Step 4:   Since the total box is empty, you should multiply.
portion size × people served = total amount of soup
8 ounces × 382 people = **3,056 ounces**

In this type of problem, the diagram can be especially helpful. The question asks how many ounces the cafeteria must make in one day. A quick reading, especially of the word "one," may be misleading. By filling in the appropriate boxes, you can see that a total is needed.

$$\begin{array}{r} 382 \\ \times\ 8 \\ \hline 3{,}056 \end{array}$$

EXERCISE 6:   For each problem, make a diagram. Then solve the problem.

　　　1.   A supermarket sold 78 cartons of Dixie cups. There were 50 cups in every carton. How many cups were sold?

2. Juanita spends an average of $6 a day for food for her family. How much did she spend during the 30-day month of June?

_____

3. The *Washington Post*'s morning edition was 140 pages long and the evening edition was 132 pages long. 780,000 copies of each edition were printed. How many pages of newsprint were needed to print the morning edition?

_____

4. A pint of floor wax covers 2,400 square feet. How many pints of floor wax are needed to wax the 168,000 square foot floor of the airline terminal?

_____

5. Fernando's car gets 18 miles per gallon. How many miles can he drive on 21 gallons of gasoline?

_____

6. 46,720 people died in car accidents last year. What was the average number of deaths each day?

_____

7. A factory produces 68,400 nails a day. 150 nails are packed in every box before shipping. How many boxes does the factory need in one day?

_____

8. During a 12-hour work day, the fast food restaurant sold 3,852 hamburgers. On the average, how many hamburgers were sold per hour?

_____

9. A seed company sold 27,429 packets of tomato seeds. If there were 35 seeds per packet, how many tomato seeds did the company sell?

_____

10. A grocery store sold 32,784 packs of cigarettes last year. The cigarettes had been shipped to the store in cartons. Each carton contained 12 packs and weighed 8 ounces. How many cartons of cigarettes were sold last year?

_____

11. There are 4 quarts in a gallon. How many quarts can be filled from a 50-gallon drum of oil?

_____

12. A football television contract for $78,000,000 is to be divided evenly among 60 colleges. How much will each college receive?

_____

Answers on page 150.

CHAPTER 6:
Multiplication And Division Word Problems With Decimals And Fractions

SOLVING DECIMAL MULTIPLICATION AND DIVISION WORD PROBLEMS

Fraction and decimal word problems are solved in the same ways as whole number word problems.

The following examples show a method for solving multiplication and division word problems containing decimals. As with whole number word problems, multiply when you are looking for the total, and divide when you are given the total and are looking for one of the parts. The approximation method can be very helpful with these problems.

Example 1:   Gasoline costs $1.499 per gallon. How much does 18 gallons of gasoline cost?

Step 1:   *question:* How much does 18 gallons of gasoline cost?

Step 2:   *necessary information:* $1.499 per gallon, 18 gallons

Step 3:   *diagram:*

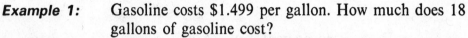

Step 4:   price of each gallon × number of gallons = total cost
18 × $1.499 = 26.982 = **$26.98**

(In money problems that have answers containing more than two decimal places, you should round off your answer to the nearest penny.)

Step 5:   *approximation:* 18 × 1.5 = 27
This approximation shows that the answer is sensible.

$$\begin{array}{r} 1.499 \\ \times\ 18 \\ \hline 26.98 \end{array}$$

Example 2:   Gil's car gets 28.6 miles per gallon. Last month he drove 943.8 miles. How many gallons of gas did he need for the month?

Step 1:   *question:* How many gallons of gas did he need for the month?

Step 2:   *necessary information:* 28.6 miles per gallon, 943.8 miles.

Step 3:   *diagram:*

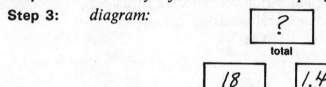

Step 4:   total miles ÷ miles per gallon = gallons
943.8 miles ÷ 28.6 miles per gallon = **33 gallons**

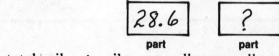

Step 5:   *approximation:* 900 ÷ 30 = 30

EXERCISE 1: For each problem, make a diagram and decide whether to multiply or divide. Then, solve the problem. Remember to write the labels of the answers and to round off all money problems to the nearest penny.

1. A runner ran an average of 6.5 minutes per mile for a race that had 242 official entrants. If the race was 6.2 miles long, how long did it take her to run it?

   _____

2. A nonprofit food co-op bought a 40-pound sack of onions for $11.60. How much will the co-op members pay per pound if the onions are sold at cost?

   _____

3. After filling her gas tank, Nancy drove 159.75 miles from Fort Lauderdale to Orlando. After the ride, her tank was filled again with 7.1 gallons of gas. On the average, how many miles per gallon did she get on the trip?

   _____

4. A beef round roast costs $2.29 per pound. How much is a 4.67 pound roast?

   _____

5. Four roommates split their food bill evenly. Last month they spent $172.36 for food and $350.00 for rent. How much did each of them pay for food?

   _____

6. A salesman, working on commission, earned $46.56 in one 8-hour workday. On the average, how much did he earn each hour?

   _____

7. A newsboy sold 304 newspapers. If each paper cost $.35, how much money did he collect?

_____

8. A diesel truck has a 60-gallon fuel tank. It gets 8.2 miles per gallon on diesel fuel. How far can it travel on a full tank of diesel fuel?

_____

Answers on page 151.

SOLVING FRACTION MULTIPLICATION WORD PROBLEMS

When you multiply two whole numbers, the answer is larger than either number. But when you multiply a number by a fraction smaller than 1, the answer is smaller than the original number; for example, $21 \times \frac{2}{3} = 14$.

Multiplication and division word problems with fractions often seem confusing. When you multiply by a fraction, you may end up with a smaller number, and when you divide by a fraction, you may end up with a larger number. This is the opposite of what you have come to expect with whole numbers.

The following chart should help you remember when to expect a larger or smaller answer when multiplying or dividing.

When multiplying a number by:	Your answer will be:	Example:
a number greater than 1	larger than the number	$36 \times 2 = 72$
1	the same as the number	$36 \times 1 = 36$
a fraction less than 1	smaller than the number	$\overset{9}{\cancel{36}} \times \frac{3}{\cancel{4}_1} = 27$

(Remember, an improper fraction is greater than 1. For example, $36 \times \frac{4}{3} = 48$.)

When dividing a number by:	Your answer will be:	Example:
a number greater than 1	smaller than the number	$36 \div 2 = \overset{18}{\cancel{36}} \times \frac{1}{\cancel{2}_1} = 18$
1	the same as the number	$36 \div 1 = 36$
a fraction smaller than 1	larger than the number	$36 \div \frac{3}{4} = \overset{12}{\cancel{36}} \times \frac{4}{\cancel{3}_1} = 48$

(Dividing by an improper fraction is the same as multiplying by a fraction less than 1. For example, $36 \div \frac{4}{3} = \overset{9}{\cancel{36}} \times \frac{3}{\cancel{4}_1} = 27$.)

The most common key word in fraction multiplication problems is "of"—as in finding a "fraction of" something. Some people confuse these problems with division because they require you to find a piece of something. The example below illustrates why you multiply when you find a fraction of a quantity.

$$\text{Find } \tfrac{1}{2} \text{ of } 6.$$

You already know that this is 3. When you multiply the two numbers you really multiply the numerators and divide by the denominator.

$$\tfrac{1}{2} \times 6 = \tfrac{1}{\cancel{2}} \times \tfrac{\cancel{6}^3}{1} = \tfrac{3}{1} = 3$$

The following examples show you how to solve multiplication word problems that require you to find a fraction of a quantity.

Example 1:   A truck is carrying $\tfrac{2}{3}$ ton of gravel. $\tfrac{1}{2}$ of this gravel is delivered to Mr. Brown. How much gravel did Mr. Brown receive?

  Step 1:   *question:* How much gravel did Mr. Brown receive?

  Step 2:   *necessary information:* $\tfrac{2}{3}$ ton, $\tfrac{1}{2}$ of this gravel

  Step 3:   *key word:* of
            fraction (of) $\times$ total = part

  Step 4: $\tfrac{1}{2} \times \tfrac{2}{3}$ ton of gravel = gravel received
            $\tfrac{1}{\cancel{2}} \times \tfrac{\cancel{2}^1}{3} = \tfrac{1}{3}$ **ton of gravel**

Example 2:   Bernie's Service Station inspected 20 cars yesterday. $\tfrac{1}{5}$ of the cars failed the inspection. How many cars failed the inspection?

  Step 1:   *question:* How many cars failed the inspection?

  Step 2:   *necessary information:* 20 cars, $\tfrac{1}{5}$ of the cars

  Step 3:   *key word:* of
            fraction (of) $\times$ total = part

  Step 4: $\tfrac{1}{5} \times 20$ cars = cars that failed
            $\tfrac{1}{\cancel{5}} \times \tfrac{\cancel{20}^4}{1} = \textbf{4 cars}$

Some fraction multiplication word problems do not have the key word "of." These problems can be recognized as multiplication since you are usually given the size of one item and asked to find the size of many. To go from one to many, you must multiply.

Example 3:   In a high school, class periods are $\frac{3}{4}$ hour long. How long is an 8-period school day?

Step 1:   *question:* How long is an 8-period school day?

Step 2:   *necessary information:* $\frac{3}{4}$ hour, 8 periods

Step 3:   You are given the length of one class period ($\frac{3}{4}$ hour) and are asked to find the total length of many class periods (8 periods). Therefore, you should multiply.

Step 4:   8 periods $\times \frac{3}{4}$ hour $= \overset{2}{\cancel{8}} \times \frac{3}{\underset{1}{\cancel{4}}} = 6 =$ **6 hours**

When you are working with a word problem and you have to decide whether to add or subtract, it is especially helpful to use Step 5: <u>Check to see that your answer is sensible.</u>

In the problem above, if you had mistakenly divided 8 by $\frac{3}{4}$, your answer would have been 12 hours. ($8 \div \frac{3}{4} = 8 \times \frac{4}{3} = 12$.) Would it make sense to say that 8 periods, each consisting of less than 1 hour each, would total 12 hours?

EXERCISE 2:   In the following exercise, underline the necessary information. Then solve the problem.

1. $\frac{2}{3}$ of the precipitation in Chicago last year was rain. Chicago had 36 inches of precipitation. How many inches of rain fell in Chicago?

   _____

2. $\frac{7}{8}$ of the car accidents in the state last year were in urban areas. There were 23,352 car accidents in the state last year. How many accidents were in urban areas?

   _____

3.   A box weighs $7\frac{2}{3}$ pounds. How much do 10 of those boxes weigh?

   _____

4.   Brad's dog Cedar eats $\frac{2}{3}$ can of dog food and 2 dog biscuits a day. How many cans of dog food will Brad need to feed Cedar for 12 days?

   _____

5. A candy bar has $1\frac{1}{8}$ ounces of peanuts. How many ounces of peanuts are in $3\frac{1}{2}$ candy bars?

_____

6. A space satellite was traveling 17,000 miles per hour. How far did it travel in $2\frac{1}{2}$ hours?

_____

7. Only $\frac{1}{2}$ cup of a new concentrated liquid detergent is needed to clean a full load of laundry. How much detergent is needed to clean $\frac{1}{2}$ of a load of laundry?

_____

8. $\frac{2}{5}$ of the hamburger meat was fat. How much fat was in a $\frac{1}{4}$-pound hamburger?

_____

Answers on page 151.

SOLVING FRACTION DIVISION WORD PROBLEMS

Remember that the second number in a fraction division problem is inverted (turned upside down). Therefore, it is very important that the total amount that is being divided is always the first number that you write in a fraction division solution. Even though the total amount must always come first when you are solving the fraction division problem, it does not always appear first in a word problem.

Example 1:   At dinner, Joyce split a $\frac{1}{4}$-pound stick of butter evenly among the 9 members of her family. How much butter did each person receive?

Step 1:   *question*: How much butter did each person receive?

Step 2:   *necessary information*: $\frac{1}{4}$ pound, 9 members

Step 3:   *key words*: split evenly, each

Many people (9) are sharing the butter. To find how much butter 1 person receives, you must divide.

total butter ÷ number of people = butter per person

Step 4: $\frac{1}{4}$ pound ÷ 9 people = $\frac{1}{4} \times \frac{1}{9}$ = **$\frac{1}{36}$ pound per person**

Many division word problems contain the concept of cutting a total into pieces. If you are given the size of the total, you must divide to find a part—either the number of pieces or the size of each piece.

Example 2:   Quality Butter Company makes butter in 60-pound batches. It then cuts each batch into $\frac{1}{4}$-pound sticks of butter. How many sticks of butter are made from each batch?

Step 1:   *question:* How many sticks of butter are made from each batch?

Step 2:   *necessary information:* 60-pound batches, $\frac{1}{4}$-pound sticks

Step 3:   *key words:* cuts, each
total amount ÷ size of each piece = number of pieces

Step 4:   60-pound batches ÷ $\frac{1}{4}$-pound sticks = $\frac{60}{1} \div \frac{1}{4} = \frac{60}{1} \times \frac{4}{1}$
= 60 × 4 = **240 sticks**

Remember: When you divide by a fraction smaller than one, your answer will be larger than the original number.

EXERCISE 3:   Underline the necessary information in each problem below. Then solve the problem.

1.   A box is $22\frac{1}{2}$ inches deep. How many books can be packed in the box if each book is $\frac{5}{8}$ inch thick?

_____

2.   Gloria is serving a dinner for 13 people. She is cooking a $6\frac{1}{2}$-pound roast. How much meat would each person get if she divided the roast evenly?

_____

3.   A bookstore giftwraps books using $2\frac{1}{4}$ feet of ribbon for each book. How many books can the store giftwrap from a roll of ribbon $265\frac{1}{2}$ feet long?

_____

4.   A container contains $8\frac{1}{2}$ pounds of mashed potatoes. Linh, who works in a cafeteria, must divide the potatoes into $\frac{1}{4}$-pound servings and the green beans into $\frac{1}{3}$-pound servings. How many servings can she make from the container of potatoes?

_____

5. One can of Diet Delight peaches contains $9\frac{3}{4}$ ounces of peaches. If one can is used for 3 equal servings, how large would each serving be?

_____

Answers on page 152.

SOLVING FRACTION MULTIPLICATION AND DIVISION
WORD PROBLEMS

EXERCISE 4: Underline the necessary information and decide whether to multiply or divide. Then solve the problem.

1. A music practice room is used 12 hours a day. If each practice session is $\frac{3}{4}$-hour long, how many sessions are there in a day?

_____

2. At full production, a car rolls off the assembly line every $\frac{2}{3}$ hour. At this rate, how long does it take to produce 30 cars?

_____

3. At full production, a car rolls off the assembly line every $\frac{2}{3}$ hour. At this rate, how many cars are produced in 24 hours?

_____

4. A consumer group claimed that $\frac{2}{3}$ of all microwave ovens were defective. 26,148 microwave ovens and 59,882 regular ovens were sold in the state last year. According to the consumer group's findings, how many microwave ovens would have been defective?

_____

5. On a wilderness hike, 6 hikers had to share $4\frac{1}{2}$ pounds of chocolate and $1\frac{3}{4}$ pounds of dry milk. If it was cut evenly, how much chocolate did each hiker receive?

_____

Answers on page 152.

REVIEW: SOLVING MULTIPLICATION AND DIVISION WORD PROBLEMS

EXERCISE 5:   For each problem, circle the letter of the correct answer. Round off money problems to the nearest penny, and other decimal problems to the nearest hundredth.

1. 40 pounds of mayonnaise were packed in jars that weighed $\frac{1}{8}$ pound and could hold $\frac{5}{8}$ pound of mayonnaise. How many jars were needed to pack all the mayonnaise?

    a. *25 jars*
    b. *64 jars*
    c. *41 jars*
    d. *320 jars*
    e. *5 jars*

2. A 32 square foot piece of $\frac{1}{4}$-inch thick plywood costs $20.80. How much does it cost per square foot?

    a. *$52.80*
    b. *$11.20*
    c. *$.65*
    d. *$12.80*
    e. *$5.20*

3. In order to cover the cost of the prizes, a VFW post had to sell at least $\frac{1}{6}$ of the raffle tickets. They had 3,000 raffle tickets printed. How many tickets did they have to sell in order to break even?

    a. *5,000 raffle tickets*
    b. *500 raffle tickets*
    c. *1,800 raffle tickets*
    d. *18,000 raffle tickets*
    e. *none of the above*

4. The trainer of the championship baseball team was voted $\frac{3}{5}$ of a winner's share. If a winner's share is $17,490, and there were 40 shares, how much money did the trainer receive?

    a. *$29,155*
    b. *$10,494*
    c. *$437.25*
    d. *$3,498*
    e. *$728.75*

5. To make one apron, Janice needed $\frac{2}{3}$ yard of cloth. She has a roll of cloth $7\frac{1}{3}$ yards long. If she doesn't waste any cloth, how many aprons can she make by cutting and using the entire roll of cloth?

   a. $4\frac{8}{9}$ aprons
   b. 4 aprons
   c. 5 aprons
   d. 11 aprons
   e. 8 aprons

6. Max used 8.1 gallons when he drove 263.1 miles in 4.5 hours. What was his average speed for the trip? (Round to the nearest tenth.)

   a. 31.1 miles per hour
   b. 58.3 miles per hour
   c. 58.4 miles per hour
   d. 58.5 miles per hour
   e. 31.2 miles per hour

7. The Motown Record Company shipped 1,410 records to the Midtown Record Store. If 30 records were packed in each box, how many boxes were needed to ship the records?

   a. 423 boxes
   b. 470 boxes
   c. 47 boxes
   d. 43 boxes
   e. none of the above

8. Ingrid ran in a 15-kilometer race. One kilometer is equal to .62 mile. How many miles did she run?

   a. 24 miles
   b. 9.3 miles
   c. 24.19 miles
   d. 4.13 miles
   e. none of the above

Answers on page 153.

CHAPTER 7:
Using Proportions: Multiplication, Division, And Conversion Word Problems

Ratios and proportions can be used to make multiplication and division problems easier to solve. Proportions can also be used to work with conversions and with percents (see Chapter 9).

WHAT ARE RATIOS?

A ratio is a comparison of two groups. Ratios can be written in a number of ways.

Example 1:   A small luncheonette has 8 chairs for 2 tables. The ratio of chairs to tables can be written three ways:

8 chairs for 2 tables
8 to 2, more commonly written as 8:2
8 chairs
2 tables

Example 2:   Marianne drove 45 miles in 3 hours on her moped. The ratio of miles to hours is written:

45 miles in 3 hours
45 to 3, or 45:3
45 miles
3 hours

In the rest of this book, you will use only the third way of writing a ratio, the fraction form.

Note: Always write a label for both the top and the bottom of the ratio.

EXERCISE 1:   In the space below, write the following relationships as ratios in the fraction form. The first problem has been done for you.

1. 1 customer bought 6 cans of tomato soup.

    1 customer
    6 cans

2. 2 teachers worked with 30 students.

3. Phi Hung earned 40 dollars in 8 hours.

4. Yvette drove 38 miles on 2 gallons of gasoline.

5. The company provided 3 buses for 114 commuters.

Answers on page 153.

WHAT ARE PROPORTIONS?

A proportion expresses that two ratios have the same value. In arithmetic, you have studied these as equivalent fractions; for example, $\frac{75}{100} = \frac{3}{4}$.

Example 1: The center of the city has 1 bus stop every 3 blocks. Therefore, the city center has 2 bus stops every 6 blocks.

$$\frac{1 \text{ bus stop}}{3 \text{ blocks}} = \frac{2 \text{ bus stops}}{6 \text{ blocks}}$$

Example 2: There are 12 ounces in 1 can of tomato sauce. Therefore, there are 48 ounces in 4 cans of tomato sauce.

$$\frac{12 \text{ ounces}}{1 \text{ can}} = \frac{48 \text{ ounces}}{4 \text{ cans}}$$

Example 3: The ratio of women to men working at the Small Motors Repair Shop is 3 women to 4 men. If there are 8 men working at the repair shop, how many women work there?

One of the numbers of the proportion is not given: the number of women working at the repair shop. Therefore, when the proportion is written, a place holder is needed in the place where the number of women should be written. The letter "n," standing for a number, is used as the place holder, but any letter could be used.

$$\frac{3 \text{ women}}{4 \text{ men}} = \frac{n \text{ women}}{8 \text{ men}}$$

Finding the number that belongs in place of the "n" is called solving a proportion. Look at two methods that can be used to solve a proportion.

METHOD 1:   **Multiplication**

Step 1:   *question:* How many women work there?

Step 2:   *necessary information:* 3 women, 4 men, 8 men

Step 3:   Write a proportion based on the problem.

$$\frac{3 \text{ women}}{4 \text{ men}} = \frac{n \text{ women}}{8 \text{ men}}$$

Notice that both denominators have been filled in and that $4 \times 2 = 8$.

$$\frac{3 \times \boxed{?}}{4 \times \boxed{2}} = \frac{n}{8}$$

Since proportions are equivalent fractions, you multiply the top and the bottom by the same number. In this problem, the number is 2.

$$\frac{3 \times \boxed{2}}{4 \times \boxed{2}} = \frac{6}{8}$$

Step 4:   Therefore, $3 \times 2 = 6$.
There are **6 women** working in the repair shop.

There are cases when Method 1: Multiplication does not work as simply. This is especially true when a problem contains a decimal, or a fraction, or the numbers are not simple multiples of each other. In these problems, Method 2: Cross Multiplication is quite useful.

METHOD 2:   **Cross Multiplication**

Step 1:   *question:* How many women work there?

Step 2:   *necessary information:* 3 women, 4 men, 8 men

Step 3:   Write the proportion.

$$\frac{3 \text{ women}}{4 \text{ men}} = \frac{n \text{ women}}{8 \text{ men}}$$

Step 4:   Cross multiply. Multiply the numbers that are on a diagonal.

Note: The letter is usually written on the left side. Also, $4n$ means the same as 4 times n. It is not necessary to write the multiplication sign, '$\times$.'

To find n, the number of women, divide the number standing alone by the number next to the letter.
n = 6 women

$$\frac{3}{4} \times \frac{n}{8}$$

$$4 \times n = 3 \times 8$$
$$4n = 24$$

$$n = \frac{24}{4} = 6$$

Notice that when you write a proportion, the labels must be consistent. For example, if "women" is the label of the top of one side of a proportion, it must be on the top of the other side.

Examples 4 and 5 below illustrate the usefulness of cross multiplication. Also, Example 4 shows the unknown, n, in the bottom of the proportion.

Example 4: Chin has seen 6 movies in the last 9 months. At this rate, how many movies will she see in 12 months?

Step 1: *question:* How many movies will she see in 12 months?

Step 2: *necessary information:* 6 movies, 9 months, 12 months

Step 3: Write the proportion.

$$\frac{12 \text{ months}}{n \text{ movies}} = \frac{9 \text{ months}}{6 \text{ movies}}$$

Step 4: Cross multiply.
Divide.

$n = 8$ **movies**

$$\frac{12}{n} \times \frac{9}{6}$$

$$9 \times n = 12 \times 6$$
$$9n = 72$$
$$n = \frac{72}{9} = 8$$

Example 5: Sandy read that she should cook a roast 20 minutes for each one-half pound. How large a roast could she cook in 90 minutes?

Step 1: *question:* How large a roast could she cook in 90 minutes?

Step 2: *necessary information:* one-half pound, 20 minutes, 90 minutes.

Step 3: Write the proportion.

$$\frac{\frac{1}{2} \text{ pound}}{20 \text{ minutes}} = \frac{n \text{ pound}}{90 \text{ minutes}}$$

Step 4: Cross multiply.
Divide.

$n = 2\frac{1}{4}$ **pounds of roast**

$$\frac{\frac{1}{2}}{20} \times \frac{n}{90}$$

$$20 \times n = 90 \times \frac{1}{2}$$
$$20n = 45$$
$$n = \frac{45}{20} = 2\frac{1}{4}$$

EXERCISE 2: Solve the following proportions for *n*.

1. $\dfrac{160 \text{ miles}}{5 \text{ hours}} = \dfrac{n \text{ miles}}{10 \text{ hours}}$

_____

2. $\dfrac{12 \text{ cars}}{32 \text{ people}} = \dfrac{3 \text{ cars}}{n \text{ people}}$

_____

3. $\dfrac{n \text{ dollars}}{8 \text{ quarters}} = \dfrac{6 \text{ dollars}}{24 \text{ quarters}}$

_____

4. $\dfrac{42 \text{ pounds}}{n \text{ chickens}} = \dfrac{14 \text{ pounds}}{4 \text{ chickens}}$

_____

5. $\dfrac{28{,}928 \text{ people}}{8 \text{ doctors}} = \dfrac{n \text{ people}}{1 \text{ doctor}}$

_____

6. $\dfrac{\$4.39}{1 \text{ shirt}} = \dfrac{n \text{ dollars}}{6 \text{ shirts}}$

_____

7. $\dfrac{\$17.85}{3 \text{ shirts}} = \dfrac{n \text{ dollars}}{10 \text{ shirts}}$

_____

8. $\dfrac{3 \text{ minutes}}{\frac{1}{2} \text{ mile}} = \dfrac{n \text{ minutes}}{5 \text{ miles}}$

_____

9. $\dfrac{575 \text{ passengers}}{n \text{ days}} = \dfrac{1{,}725 \text{ passengers}}{21 \text{ days}}$

_____

10. $\dfrac{7 \text{ blinks}}{\frac{1}{10} \text{ minute}} = \dfrac{n \text{ blinks}}{10 \text{ minutes}}$

_____

Answers on page 153.

USING PROPORTIONS TO SOLVE
MULTIPLICATION AND DIVISION WORD PROBLEMS

Multiplication and division word problems can be solved using proportions.

The following examples show how to write proportions to solve multiplication word problems.

Example 1: There are 16 cups in a gallon. At the church picnic, Carmella poured 5 gallons of Coke into paper cups that each held 1 cup of soda. How many cups did she fill?

Step 1: *question:* How many cups did she fill?

Step 2: *necessary information:* 16 cups in a gallon, 5 gallons, 1 cup.

Step 3: Write the proportion.

labels for proportion: $\dfrac{\text{cups}}{\text{gallon}}$

$$\frac{16 \text{ cups}}{1 \text{ gallon}} = \frac{n \text{ cups}}{5 \text{ gallons}}$$

Step 4: Cross multiply.

(*n* means the same as $1 \times n$. From now on you don't need to write the 1 and the "×" sign, so you write n = 16×5.)

n = 80 cups

$$\frac{16}{1} \times \frac{n}{5}$$

$$n = 16 \times 5$$
$$n = 80$$

Remember: When writing the labels for a proportion, it doesn't matter which category goes on top. But once you make a decision, you must stick with it. Once you put "cups" on the top of one ratio, you must keep "cups" on top of the other.

16 cups in a gallon means the same as $\dfrac{16 \text{ cups}}{1 \text{ gallon}}$. The 1 will often not appear in these word problems. When writing a proportion, you must determine when a 1 is needed and where it goes. You can do this by first identifying the two labels and then putting numbers in the proportion.

There are a number of word phrases that require that a 1 be used in a ratio. Some examples are:

Phrases	Meaning
27 miles per gallon	$\dfrac{27 \text{ miles}}{1 \text{ gallon}}$
$8 an hour	$\dfrac{\$8}{1 \text{ hour}}$
3 meals a day	$\dfrac{3 \text{ meals}}{1 \text{ day}}$
30 miles each day	$\dfrac{30 \text{ miles}}{1 \text{ day}}$

Example 2:   A factory shipped out 84 carburetors. Each carburetor weighed 9 pounds. What was the total weight of the shipment?

Step 1:   *question:* What is the total weight of the shipment?

Step 2:   *necessary information:* 84 carburetors, 9 pounds

Step 3:   *labels for proportion:* $\dfrac{\text{carburetors}}{\text{pounds}}$

$\dfrac{84 \text{ carburetors}}{n \text{ pounds}} = \dfrac{1 \text{ carburetor}}{9 \text{ pounds}}$

$$\frac{84}{n} \diagup\!\!\!\diagdown \frac{1}{9}$$

Step 4:   Cross multiply.

$n = $ **756 pounds**

$$n = 84 \times 9$$
$$n = 756$$

Example 3:   At the Boardwalk Arcade, owner Manuel Santos collects 1,380 quarters every day. There are 4 quarters in a dollar. How many dollars does he collect every day?

Step 1:   *question:* How many dollars does he collect every day?

Step 2:   *necessary information:* 1,380 quarters, 4 quarters in a dollar

$$\frac{n}{1,380} \diagup\!\!\!\diagdown \frac{1}{4}$$

Step 3:   *labels for proportion:* $\dfrac{\text{dollars}}{\text{quarters}}$

$\dfrac{n \text{ dollars}}{1,380 \text{ quarters}} = \dfrac{1 \text{ dollar}}{4 \text{ quarters}}$

Step 4:   Cross multiply.

$$4 \times n = 1,380 \times 1$$
$$4n = 1,380$$

Divide.

$n = $ **345 dollars**

$$n = \frac{1,380}{4} = 345$$

EXERCISE 3:   Underline the necessary information. Write proportions for the problems below and then solve them.

1. A shipment of vaccine can protect 7,800 people. How many shipments of vaccine are needed to protect 140,400 people living in the Portland area?

    _____

2. It costs $340 an hour to run the 1,000–watt power generator. How much does it cost to run the generator for 24 hours?

    _____

3. There are 11 ounces in a can of soup. How many ounces of soup are in a carton containing 28 cans?

    _____

4. Jim can type 52 words per minute. How many words did he type when he typed for 26 minutes?

_____

5. An elementary school nurse used 3,960 Band-Aids last year. There were 180 school days. On the average, how many Band-Aids did he use a day?

_____

6. The company health clinic gave out 5,460 aspirins and 720 antacid tablets last year. How many bottles of aspirin did the clinic use last year if there were 260 aspirins in a bottle?

_____

7. A coal mine produced 126 tons of slag in a week. Trucks removed the slag in three-ton loads. How many trips were needed to remove all the slag?

_____

8. Cloth is sold by the yard. Edyth needs to buy 18 feet of cloth to make dresses. There are 3 feet in a yard. How many yards of cloth should she buy?

_____

9. A six-ounce can of waterchestnuts contains 26 waterchestnuts. Hong used three cans of waterchestnuts. How many waterchestnuts did she use?

_____

Answers on page 154.

USING PROPORTIONS TO SOLVE DECIMAL
MULTIPLICATION AND DIVISION WORD PROBLEMS

You can use proportions to solve decimal multiplication and division word problems. The problems should be set up as if the numbers were whole numbers. Multiply or divide as if you were dealing with whole numbers. Then use the rules for decimal multiplication and division to place the decimal point in the right place. Finally, round off the answer if necessary.

Example 1:   Ray has $15.00 to spend on gasoline. How many gallons can he buy if one gallon costs $1.20?

Step 1:   *question:* How many gallons can he buy?

Step 2:   *necessary information:* $15.00, $1.20

Step 3:   *labels for proportion:* $\dfrac{\$}{\text{gallon}}$

$$\frac{\$15.00}{n \text{ gallons}} = \frac{\$1.20}{1 \text{ gallon}}$$

Step 4:   Cross multiply.
Divide.
n = **12.5 gallons**

$$\frac{15}{n} = \frac{1.20}{1}$$

$$1.20 \times n = 15 \times 1$$
$$1.20n = 15$$

$$n = \frac{15}{1.20} = 12.5$$

Example 2:   There are 236.5 milliliters in a cup. A recipe called for 3 cups of flour. Maria only has metric spoons and measuring cups. How many milliliters of flour does she need for the recipe?

Step 1:   *question:* How many milliliters of flour does she need for the recipe?

Step 2:   *necessary information:* 236.5 milliliters in a cup, 3 cups

Step 3:   *labels for proportion:* $\dfrac{\text{milliliters}}{\text{cups}}$

$$\frac{236.5 \text{ milliliters}}{1 \text{ cup}} = \frac{n \text{ milliliters}}{3 \text{ cups}}$$

Step 4:   Cross multiply.
n = **709.5 milliliters**

$$\frac{236.5}{1} = \frac{n}{3}$$
$$n = 3 \times 236.5$$
$$n = 709.5$$

EXERCISE 4:   Underline the necessary information. Write the labels for the proportion, fill in the numbers, and then solve it. Round your answers to the nearest hundredth.

1.   There are 25.4 millimeters in an inch. How many inches long is a 100 millimeter cigarette?

_____

2.   A kilogram weighs 2.2 pounds. The police seized 36 kilograms of illegal drugs. How many pounds did the drugs weigh?

_____

3.   Alba worked 35.5 hours last week. She earns $4.62 an hour. How much money did she earn last week?

_____

4.   There are 1.09 yards in a meter. Gary ran in an 880-yard race. How many meters did he run?

_____

5.   Caroline spent $20 on gasoline. The gasoline cost $1.15 per gallon. How many gallons of gasoline did she buy?

_____

6.   There are 1.61 kilometers in a mile. The speedometer on Iris's imported car is in kilometers per hour. She does not want to speed. What is 55 miles per hour in kilometers per hour?

_____

Answers on page 155.

USING PROPORTIONS TO SOLVE FRACTION MULTIPLICATION AND DIVISION WORD PROBLEMS

Proportions can be used to solve multiplication and division word problems containing fractions. Though they look complicated when you set them up, they are manageable after you cross multiply.

Example 1:   A dump truck can carry a load of $2\frac{3}{4}$ tons of gravel. In one day, the truck removed 8 loads of gravel from a gravel pit. How many tons of gravel did it remove from the pit that day?

Step 1:   *question:* How many tons of gravel did it remove from the pit that day?

Step 2:   *necessary information:* a load of $2\frac{3}{4}$ tons, 8 loads

Step 3:   *labels for proportion:* $\dfrac{\text{tons}}{\text{loads}}$

$$\frac{2\frac{3}{4}\ \text{tons}}{1\ \text{load}} = \frac{n\ \text{tons}}{8\ \text{loads}}$$

$$\frac{2\frac{3}{4}}{1} \times \frac{n}{8}$$

Step 4:   Cross multiply.

$n = 22$ **tons**

$$n = 8 \times 2\frac{3}{4}$$

$$n = \overset{2}{8} \times \frac{11}{\underset{1}{4}} = 22$$

Example 2:   Burger King makes a $\frac{1}{4}$-pound hamburger. How many of these hamburgers can be made from 50 pounds of hamburger meat?

Step 1:   *question:* How many of these hamburgers can be made?

Step 2:   *necessary information:* $\frac{1}{4}$ pound, 50 pounds

Step 3:   *labels for proportion:* $\dfrac{\text{pounds}}{\text{hamburgers}}$

$$\frac{\frac{1}{4}\ \text{pound}}{1\ \text{hamburger}} = \frac{50\ \text{pounds}}{n\ \text{hamburgers}}$$

$$\frac{\frac{1}{4}}{1} \times \frac{50}{n}$$

Step 4:   Cross multiply.

$n = 200$ **hamburgers**

$$\frac{1}{4} \times n = 50 \times 1$$

$$\frac{1}{4}n = 50$$

$$n = 50 \times 4 = 200$$

A word problem asking you to find a fraction of something is easier to solve by direct multiplication rather than by using a proportion. Example 3 illustrates this.

Example 3: $\frac{2}{5}$ of all gallons of milk sold in a store are low-fat. The store sold 380 gallons of milk. How many gallons of low-fat milk were sold?

You could set up the following proportion to solve the problem:

$$\frac{\frac{2}{5} \text{ low-fat}}{1 \text{ gallon}} = \frac{n \text{ low-fat}}{380 \text{ gallons}}$$

While this will give you the correct answer, it is easier to remember that you should multiply to find a fraction of something. It is easier to solve the problem this way:

fraction (of) × total gallons = low-fat gallons

$$\frac{2}{\cancel{5}_1} \times \frac{\cancel{380}^{76}}{1} = \frac{2}{1} \times \frac{76}{1} = \textbf{152 gallons}$$

EXERCISE 5:   Underline the necessary information. Write the proportions and solve the problems below.

1.   A slicing machine cut roast beef $\frac{1}{16}$ inch thick. The giant sandwich was advertised to have roast beef 2 inches thick on it. How many slices of roast beef were on the sandwich?

   _____

2.   A Baby Ruth candy bar weighs $1\frac{5}{8}$ ounces. The Sweets Vending Machine Company stocked one of its machines with 60 Baby Ruth candy bars and 50 Hershey chocolate bars. How many ounces of Baby Ruth candy bars were in the machine?

   _____

3.   The La Ronga Bakery baked 1,460 loaves of bread in one day. If each loaf contained $1\frac{3}{4}$ teaspoons salt, how much salt was used by the bakery?

   _____

4.   How many books $\frac{7}{8}$ inch thick can be packed in a box 35 inches deep?

   _____

5. A can of pears weighs $9\frac{2}{3}$ ounces. There are 16 cans of pears in a carton. How many ounces does a carton of pears weigh?

_____

6. There are 8 cups of detergent in a bottle of Easy Clean Detergent. $\frac{1}{4}$ cup is all that is needed for one load of laundry. How many loads of laundry can be cleaned with a bottle of Easy Clean?

_____

7. There are 160 pea pods in a pound. Tung-mei used $\frac{1}{4}$ pound of pea pods when she made vegetables and rice. How many pea pods did she use?

_____

Answers on page 156.

SOLVING CONVERSION WORD PROBLEMS

Have you ever seen this kind of problem?

Example: Caren has a 204-inch roll of masking tape. How many feet of molding can she cover with the roll?

This problem is an example of a type of multiplication or division word problem that contains only one number and requires outside information in order to be solved. These are word problems involving conversions from one type of measurement to another.

Here is the solution and explanation of the example:

Step 1:   *question*: How many feet?

Step 2:   *necessary information*: 204 inches

Notice that the question asks for a solution that has a different label than what is given in the problem. To solve this, you must know how to convert inches to feet. Then you can set up a proportion to solve the problem.

Step 3:   12 inches = 1 foot

labels for proportion: $\dfrac{\text{inches}}{\text{feet}}$

The conversion will be one side of the proportion.

$$\frac{12 \text{ inches}}{1 \text{ foot}} = \frac{204 \text{ inches}}{n \text{ feet}}$$

Step 4:   Cross multiply.

$$\frac{12}{1} \diagup\!\!\!\times\!\!\!\diagdown \frac{204}{n}$$

$$12 \times n = 204 \times 1$$

$$12n = 204$$

Divide.
n = 17 feet

$$n = \frac{204}{12} = 17$$

There are many word problems that cannot be solved unless you know a conversion. Here are lists of some common measurements and their conversions.

Time Conversions

365 days = 1 year

12 months = 1 year

52 weeks = 1 year

7 days = 1 week

24 hours = 1 day

60 minutes = 1 hour

60 seconds = 1 minute

Length and Area Conversions

5,280 feet = 1 mile

1,760 yards = 1 mile

3 feet = 1 yard

36 inches = 1 yard

12 inches = 1 foot

144 square inches = 1 square foot

1,000 meters = 1 kilometer

100 centimeters = 1 meter

1,000 millimeters = 1 meter

10 millimeters = 1 centimeter

Weight Conversions

2,000 pounds = 1 ton

16 ounces = 1 pound

1,000 grams = 1 kilogram

1,000 milligrams = 1 gram

Volume Conversions

4 quarts = 1 gallon

2 pints = 1 quart

2 cups = 1 pint

32 ounces = 1 quart

16 ounces = 1 pint

8 ounces = 1 cup

1,000 milliliters = 1 liter

EXERCISE 6:   Write the conversion and the proportion. Then solve the problem.

1. How many years old was Gloria's 30 month old daughter?

   _____

2. A 200-gallon batch of ketchup was bottled in quart bottles. How many bottles were filled?

   _____

3. How many kilometers long is a 10,000-meter road race?

   _____

4. Paul's truck can carry a $\frac{1}{2}$-ton load. How many pounds of gravel can it carry?

   _____

5. José brought 3 quarts of cream to the outing. How many ounces of cream did he bring?

   _____

6. Mt. Everest is 29,028 feet high. How many miles high is Mt. Everest? (Round off to the nearest tenth.)

   _____

Answers on page 156.

USING PROPORTIONS TO SOLVE MULTIPLICATION AND DIVISION WORD PROBLEMS CONTAINING BOTH A FRACTION AND A DECIMAL

Sometimes you will find a multiplication or division word problem in which one number is a decimal and the other is a fraction. The proportion method is very useful in solving this type of word problem.

Example: A $\frac{3}{4}$-pound steak cost \$6.75. How much did it cost per pound?

Step 1:   *question:* How much did it cost per pound?

Step 2:   *necessary information:* $\frac{3}{4}$ pound, \$6.75

Step 3:   *labels for proportion:* pound, \$

$$\frac{\frac{3}{4} \text{ pound}}{\$6.75} = \frac{1 \text{ pound}}{n \text{ dollars}}$$

Step 4:   Cross multiply.
Divide.
$n = \$9.00$

$$\frac{\frac{3}{4}}{6.75} \times \frac{1}{n}$$

$$\frac{3}{4} n = 6.75$$

$$n = 6.75 \times \frac{4}{3}$$

$$n = 9.00$$

If you had not been able to cancel in the above problem, you would have multiplied the numerators (tops) and divided by the denominators (bottoms). Be careful to keep the decimal point in the correct place.

EXERCISE 7:   Write the proportions and solve the problems below. (Round off money problems to the nearest penny.)

1. Cloth was being sold at \$12.60 a yard. Lori bought $3\frac{1}{3}$ yards of cloth. How much did she spend?

   _____

2. 13.5 pounds of time-release fertilizer is supposed to last $4\frac{1}{2}$ years. How much fertilizer is used up each year?

   _____

3. Murray bought $2\frac{2}{3}$ pounds of grapes for \$3.25. How much did the grapes cost per pound?

   _____

4. Marty took pictures at graduation. He used $7\frac{1}{2}$ rolls of film, and charged $384.50. What was the charge per roll of film?

_____

Answers on page 157.

USING PROPORTIONS TO SOLVE MULTIPLICATION AND DIVISION WORD PROBLEMS

EXERCISE 8:   Underline the necessary information. Write the proportions and then solve the problems below.

1.   A butcher can cut up a chicken in $\frac{1}{12}$ of an hour. How many chickens can he cut up in an 8-hour work day?

_____

2.   A nurse can take 8 blood samples in 60 minutes. How long does it take her to take one blood sample?

_____

3.   A mile is 1.6 kilometers. How many kilometers is a 26-mile marathon?

_____

4.   An oil drilling rig can drill 6 feet in an hour. How far can it drill in 24 hours?

_____

5   A gram is .04 ounce. How many grams are in a 12-ounce can of pineapple juice?

_____

6. Rose uses $3\frac{1}{4}$ pounds of pumpkin to make two pumpkin pies. For a fall bake sale, she made 10 pies. How many pounds of pumpkin did she use?

_____

7. When the floodgates were opened, 68,000 gallons of water flowed over the dam per hour. How many gallons flowed over the dam in a day?

_____

8. Lace trimming costs $.12 per foot. How much did Zelda spend on $4\frac{1}{4}$ feet of trimming?

_____

9. Superglue sets in $3\frac{1}{2}$ minutes. In how many seconds does Superglue set?

_____

10. A 942-page book contained 302,382 words. On the average, how many words were on each page?

_____

Answers on page 157.

CHAPTER 8:
Mixed Word Problems

So far, you have worked with word problems that have been divided into two major categories—addition/subtraction type problems and multiplication/division type problems.

In most situations, you will be faced with the four types of problems mixed together. Always read each problem carefully to get an understanding of the situation it describes. This will help you to choose the right arithmetic.

Keep these general guidelines in mind:

- when combining amounts ─────────────────► add
- when finding the difference between two amounts ─────────────────────────► subtract
- when given one unit of something and asked to find several ──────────────────────────► multiply
- when asked to find a fraction (of) a quantity─► multiply
- when given the amount for several and asked for one ────────────────────────────► divide
- when splitting, cutting, sharing, etc.─────► divide

Working through the following exercises will help to sharpen your skills with word problems when the different types are mixed together. In Exercise 1, you will be asked to recognize the type of problem without solving it. Exercise 2 involves solving problems containing only whole numbers, and Exercise 3 gives you an opportunity to work with whole numbers, decimals, and fractions.

___

MIXED WORD PROBLEMS WITH WHOLE NUMBERS

EXERCISE 1:   On the line below each problem, write the arithmetic operation that you would use to solve it: addition, subtraction, multiplication, or division. DO NOT SOLVE!

1. A ream of paper contains 500 sheets. A box contains 10 reams of paper. How many sheets of paper are in the box?

_____

2. After taxes, Emmanuel earned $13,560. He had paid $1,280 in taxes. What was his total income for the year?

_____

3. It costs $3 to go to the movies. A movie theatre collected $261 in ticket sales. How many tickets were sold?

_____

4. A department store bought shirts for $4 each and sold them for $8. How much profit did they make on each shirt?

_____

5. Tom needs 19 feet of molding for each doorway in his home. The home will have 9 doorways. How much molding does he need?

_____

6. On Wednesday, Rob harvested 476 ears of corn and 94 zucchini. On Thursday, he harvested 548 ears of corn and 129 zucchini. How many more ears of corn did he harvest on Thursday?

_____

7. The sale sign said, "Marked down $5." If a shirt cost $21, what was its original price?

_____

8. A fisherman reeled in his line 56 times while he was fishing. If he fished for 8 hours, how many times did he reel in his line hourly (on an average)?

_____

Answers on page 158.

EXERCISE 2:   In the following problems, decide whether to add, subtract, multiply, or divide and then solve. Circle the letter of the correct answer.

1 Mr. Gomez's obituary appeared in a 1983 newspaper. It said that he was 86 years old when he died and had been married 51 years. In what year was he born?

a. 1903
b. 1932
c. 1869
d. 1887
e. 1897

2. 4 roommates divided their rent evenly. If they each paid $140 a month, how much did the entire apartment cost?

a. $144
b. $136
c. $35
d. $30
e. $560

3. A ferry can carry a maximum of 35 cars at one time. If it makes 7 trips in one day, what is the maximum number of cars that it can carry?

a. 5 cars
b. 28 cars
c. 42 cars
d. 245 cars
e. 490 cars

4. The population of San Jose rose by 37,290 people. The population had been 596,640. What was the new population?

a. 559,350 people
b. 633,930 people
c. 160,000 people
d. 180,500 people
e. none of the above

5. A Christmas light uses 2 watts of electricity. How many lights can be strung on a circuit that can handle a load of 300 watts?

a. 150 lights
b. 600 lights
c. 298 lights
d. 302 lights
e. none of the above

6. A telephone cable can handle 12,500 calls at any one time. How many cables are needed to handle a peak load of 87,500 calls?

   a. *100,000 cables*
   b. *75,000 cables*
   c. *7 cables*
   d. *70 cables*
   e. *none of the above*

7. Gene bought $360 of sports equipment for the boys club. Since the boys club is tax exempt, he didn't have to pay the $18 sales tax. If he had paid tax, how much would he have spent?

   a. *$20*
   b. *$200*
   c. *$342*
   d. *$360*
   e. *$378*

8. A clothing factory produced 8,760 yards of cloth. What was the average production from each of the 60 looms in the factory?

   a. *146 yards*
   b. *1,460 yards*
   c. *8,700 yards*
   d. *8,820 yards*
   e. *525,600 yards*

9. Len's goal was to sell 20 encyclopedias a month. During his best month, he sold 37 encyclopedias. By how much did he exceed his goal?

   a. *57 encyclopedias*
   b. *17 encyclopedias*
   c. *13 encyclopedias*
   d. *2 encyclopedias*
   e. *740 encyclopedias*

10. A farm produced 91,035 ears of corn. On the average, each ear contained 315 kernels. How many kernels of corn were produced at the farm?

    a. *91,350 kernels*
    b. *90,720 kernels*
    c. *289 kernels*
    d. *28,676,025 kernels*
    e. *none of the above*

Answers on page 158.

MIXED WORD PROBLEMS—WHOLE NUMBERS, DECIMALS AND FRACTIONS

EXERCISE 3:   For all problems, circle the correct answer. Decimals are to be rounded off to the nearest penny or the nearest hundredth.

1. Sandy bought a roast beef sandwich for $1.89, which included $.09 tax. What was the cost of the sandwich alone?

   a. *$1.89*
   b. *$1.80*
   c. *$1.98*
   d. *$2.10*
   e. *$1.70*

2. The population of the United States was 213,478,921. The population of the Soviet Union was 231,300,845. How much greater was the population of the Soviet Union?

   a. *17,821,924 people*
   b. *444,779,766 people*
   c. *22,178,124 people*
   d. *444,778,766 people*
   e. *none of the above*

3. To tie her tomatoes, Emmy cut a 12-foot string into $\frac{3}{4}$-foot-long pieces. How many pieces of string did she then have to tie her tomatoes?

   a. *$12\frac{3}{4}$ feet*
   b. *$11\frac{1}{4}$ feet*
   c. *9 pieces*
   d. *16 pieces*
   e. *none of the above*

4. The auto repair shop charged Muriel $1,125 to repair her car. She had a $250 deductible insurance policy. How much did the insurance company pay for the repair of her car?

   a. *$1,375*
   b. *$875*
   c. *$4.50*
   d. *$281.25*
   e. *none of the above*

5. Chicken costs $.65 a pound. Cali paid $2.90 for a cut up chicken. How much did the chicken weigh? (round to nearest hundredth)

   a. *2.25 pounds*
   b. *2.35 pounds*
   c. *1.89 pounds*
   d. *4.46 pounds*
   e. *18.90 pounds*

6. A strobe light flashes every $\frac{1}{250}$ of a second. How many times does it flash in 5 seconds?

   a. *50 times*
   b. *1,250 times*
   c. *250 times*
   d. $4\frac{249}{250}$ *times*
   e. $5\frac{1}{250}$ *times*

7. Amanda packed 16 ounces of dried chives into bottles. Each bottle was $3\frac{1}{2}$ inches high and contained $\frac{5}{8}$ ounce of chives. How many bottles did she use?

   a. *10 bottles*
   b. *25 bottles*
   c. $16\frac{5}{8}$ *bottles*
   d. *56 bottles*
   e. *none of the above*

8. The Concorde flew 3,855 miles across the Atlantic in $3\frac{3}{4}$ hours. What was its average speed?

   a. $3,858\frac{3}{4}$ *miles per hour*
   b. $3,851\frac{1}{4}$ *miles per hour*
   c. *1,028 miles per hour*
   d. $14,456\frac{1}{3}$ *miles per hour*
   e. $467\frac{9}{33}$ *miles per hour*

9. Mary spent $\frac{1}{3}$ of her paycheck on food and $\frac{1}{4}$ for clothes. Her check was for $174. How much did she spend for food?

   a. *$43.75*
   b. *$25*
   c. *$51.40*
   d. *$58*
   e. *$4.38*

10. The city school system planned to lay off 216 teachers and 85 aides. How many people was the school system planning to lay off?

   a. *131 people*
   b. *171 people*
   c. *301 people*
   d. *271 people*
   e. *3 people*

11. The Platte River is normally 7 feet deep. During a recent flood it crested at 14 feet above normal. What was the depth of the river at the crest of the flood?

   a. *7 feet*
   b. *21 feet*
   c. *98 feet*
   d. *2 feet*
   e. *none of the above*

12. A stick of butter weighs $\frac{1}{4}$ pound. A recipe calls for $\frac{1}{2}$ stick of butter. How many pounds of butter are called for in the recipe?

   a. *2 pounds*
   b. *$\frac{3}{4}$ pound*
   c. *$\frac{1}{4}$ pound*
   d. *$\frac{1}{8}$ pound*
   e. *$\frac{1}{2}$ pound*

13. A wooden board is $\frac{7}{8}$ inch thick. To fit into a groove, it must be $\frac{13}{16}$ inch thick. How much of the board must be sanded off for it to fit in the groove?

   a. *$\frac{3}{4}$ inch*
   b. *$\frac{5}{6}$ inch*
   c. *$1\frac{1}{13}$ inch*
   d. *$1\frac{11}{16}$ inch*
   e. *$\frac{1}{16}$ inch*

14. Rene had to ship a 3.6 pound package. Overnight Delivery Service charged $1.16 per pound for the delivery. How much did Rene pay to get her package delivered?

   a. *$4.76*
   b. *$2.44*
   c. *$2.56*
   d. *$4.18*
   e. *$3.10*

15. A public television station expected private contributions to pay for $\frac{2}{3}$ of its expenses. Before the end-of-year appeal, these contributions totaled only enough to pay for $\frac{4}{9}$ of expenses. How much more must be raised in the year-end appeal?

   a. $\frac{2}{9}$ of expenses
   b. $\frac{1}{2}$ of expenses
   c. $\frac{1}{3}$ of expenses
   d. $\frac{6}{27}$ of expenses
   e. $\frac{2}{3}$ of expenses

16. A factory produces 4-ton steel girders. How much steel does the factory need to produce 1,200 of these girders?

   a. 300 tons
   b. 4,800 tons
   c. 1,204 tons
   d. 1,196 tons
   e. none of the above

17. After getting a tune-up, Ernie was able to drive 283.1 miles on 14.9 gallons of gas. How many miles did he get per gallon?

   a. 19 miles
   b. 42.18 miles
   c. 134 miles
   d. 298 miles
   e. 268.2 miles

18. Harry sanded $\frac{1}{6}$ of a floor. Fran sanded $\frac{1}{4}$ of the floor. How much of the floor got sanded?

   a. $\frac{1}{5}$ of the floor
   b. $\frac{2}{3}$ of the floor
   c. $\frac{5}{12}$ of the floor
   d. $\frac{1}{12}$ of the floor
   e. $\frac{1}{24}$ of the floor

19. A cake recipe called for 3 cups of flour. If Ida wants to make $\frac{1}{2}$ of the recipe, how much flour will she need?

   a. $3\frac{1}{2}$ cups
   b. $2\frac{1}{2}$ cups
   c. $1\frac{1}{2}$ cups
   d. $\frac{2}{3}$ cup
   e. 6 cups

20. A newsboy sold 304 newspapers. If each newspaper costs $.35, how much money did he collect?

    a. *$106.40*
    b. *$86.86*
    c. *$304.35*
    d. *$303.65*
    e. *none of the above*

21. A bunch of grapes weighed 1.84 pounds. Another bunch of grapes weighed 2.2 pounds. How much heavier was the second bunch of grapes?

    a. *1.62 pounds*
    b. *2.06 pounds*
    c. *4.05 pounds*
    d. *4.04 pounds*
    e. *.36 pound*

22. A package of peaches weighed 1.72 pounds. A package of plums weighed .9 pound. What was the total weight of the two packages?

    a. *1.81 pounds*
    b. *1.63 pounds*
    c. *2.62 pounds*
    d. *1.55 pounds*
    e. *.82 pound*

23. At the New York Stock Market, a stock opened at $20\frac{3}{8}$ a share and closed at the end of the day at $22\frac{1}{2}$. How much did it gain for the day?

    a. *$42\frac{7}{8}$*
    b. *$2\frac{1}{8}$*
    c. *$2\frac{1}{3}$*
    d. *$2\frac{2}{5}$*
    e. *none of the above*

24. Kendra deposited $28 in her Christmas Club account every week for a year. How much money did she deposit in the account?

    a. *$24*
    b. *$80*
    c. *$336*
    d. *$1,456*
    e. *none of the above*

Answers on page 159.

CHAPTER 9:
Percent Word Problems

IDENTIFYING THE PARTS OF A PERCENT WORD PROBLEM

Read the statement below:

The 8-ounce glass is 50% full. It contains 4 ounces.

This statement contains three facts:

the whole: the 8-ounce glass
the part: 4 ounces
the percent: 50%

A percent word problem would be missing one of these facts. When solving a percent word problem, the first step is to identify what you are looking for. As shown above, you have three possible choices: *the part*, *the whole*, or *the percent*.

It is usually easiest to figure out that you are being asked to find the percent. Word problems asking for the percent usually ask for it directly with such questions as, "What is the percent?" or "Find the percent," or "3 is what percent?" Occasionally, other percent-type words are used, such as "What is the *interest rate*?"

Example 1: 6 is what percent of 30?

The question asks, "is what percent?" Therefore, you are looking for the percent.

Sometimes you are given the percent and one other number. You must decide whether you are looking for the part or the whole.

Example 2: 81% of what number is 162?

The phrase "of what number" means you are looking for the whole.

Example 3: 114 city employees were absent yesterday. This was 4% of the city work force. How many people work for the city?

Step 1: *question:* How many people work for the city?

Step 2: *necessary information:* 114 city employees, 4%

Step 3: You are given the number of city employees who were absent (114) and the percent of the work force that this represents (4%). You are looking for the total number of the people who work for the city, the whole.

Example 4:   What number is 75% of 40?
You are looking for a number that is a percent of another number. You are looking for the part.

Example 5:   Operating at full capacity, the automobile plant produced 25 cars an hour. How many cars did the plant produce when operating at 40% capacity?

Step 1:   *question:* How many cars did the plant produce?

Step 2:   *necessary information:* 25 cars, 40%

Step 3:   You are given the production at full capacity (25 cars an hour). To find the production at 40% capacity, you must solve for the part.

EXERCISE 1:   For each problem, write down whether you are looking for the part, the whole, or the percent. DO NOT SOLVE!!

1. The city reported that 14,078 out of 35,817 registered voters voted in the election. What percent of the registered voters voted in the election?

   _____

2. The winning candidate won 54% of the total vote of 14,615. How many votes did she get?

   _____

3. 36% of the plumbers polled recommended Drāno. 72 plumbers recommended Drāno. How many plumbers were polled?

   _____

4. 85% of Eric's roll of 36 pictures were perfect prints. How many perfect prints did he get from the roll?

   _____

5. A seed company guaranteed 87% germination of its spinach seed. If Jed had 450 spinach seeds germinate, how many seeds did he plant?

    _____

6. The state had a work force of 1,622,145. 132,998 of those people were unemployed. What was the unemployment rate for the state?

    _____

7. A bedroom set normally priced at $1,400 is on sale for 40% off. How much would Rochelle save if she bought the set on sale instead of at the regular price?

    _____

8. Last year, 980 people took the high school equivalency exam at the local official test center. 637 people passed the exam. What percent of the people taking the exam passed?

    _____

9. If 8% of the registered voters sign the initiative petition, it will be placed on the November ballot. There are 193,825 registered voters in the county. How many of them must sign the petition for it to go on the ballot?

    _____

10. An independent study group estimated that only 35% of all crimes in the city were reported. There were 2,800 reported crimes last year. According to the study, how many crimes were actually committed?

    _____

Answers on page 159.

SOLVING PERCENT WORD PROBLEMS

Once you identify what you are looking for in a percent word problem, set up the problem and solve it.

Percent word problems can be solved using proportions. These problems can be set up in the following form:

$$\frac{\text{part}}{\text{whole}} = \frac{\%}{100\%}$$

Using the proportion method, you can solve for one of three numbers: the part, the whole, or the percent. The percent is always written over 100 because the percent represents a fraction with 100 in the denominator.

As you saw in your earlier work with proportions, a proportion is the same as two equivalent fractions. For example, 2 is 50% of 4 and can be written as

$$\frac{2}{4} = \frac{50\%}{100\%}$$

2 is the *part*, 4 is the *whole*, and 50 is the *percent*.

Example 1:   4 is what percent of 16?

Step 1:   *question:* is what percent?
You are looking for the percent.

Step 2:   *necessary information:* 4 is, of 16
For this type of percent exercise, the word "is" follows the part, and the number after "of" is the whole.

Step 3:   Set up a proportion in this form:

numbers   *percents*

$$\frac{\text{part}}{\text{whole}} = \frac{\text{percent}}{100}$$

Fill in the proportion with the given information from the problem. Call the number you are looking for "*n*."

numbers   *percents*

$$\frac{4}{16} = \frac{n}{100}$$

Step 4:   Cross multiply: $16 \times n = 4 \times 100$
$$16n = 400$$
Divide: $n = \frac{400}{16} = 25\%$

Example 2:   24 out of 96 city playgrounds needed major repairs. What percent of the city playgrounds needed major repairs?

Step 1:   *question:* What percent of the city playgrounds needed major repairs?
You are looking for the percent.

Step 2:   *necessary information:* 24 out of 96 city playgrounds
96 is the whole (all the playgrounds)
24 is the part (playgrounds needing repairs)

Step 3:   <u>numbers</u>   <u>percents</u>

$$\frac{24 \text{ playgrounds}}{96 \text{ playgrounds}} = \frac{n}{100}$$

Step 4:   Cross multiply: $96 \times n = 24 \times 100$

$$96n = 2,400$$

Divide: $n = \dfrac{2,400}{96} = \mathbf{25.\%}$

Example 3:   30% of what number is 78?

Step 1:   *question:* of what number?
You are looking for the whole.

Step 2:   *necessary information:* 30%, is 78
30% is the percent.
78 is the part.

Step 3:   Set up a proportion in this form:

<u>numbers</u>   <u>percents</u>

$$\frac{78}{n} = \frac{30}{100}$$

Step 4:   Cross multiply: $30 \times n = 78 \times 100$

$$30n = 7,800$$

Divide: $n = \dfrac{7,800}{30} = \mathbf{260}$

Example 4:   The finance company required that Lynn make a down payment of 15% on a used car. She can afford a down payment of $600. What is the most expensive car that she could buy?

Step 1:   *question:* What is the most expensive car that she could buy?
You are looking for the whole (the price of the car).

Step 2:   *necessary information:* 15%, $600
15% is the percent.
$600 is the down payment, which is a part of the total price of the car.

<u>numbers</u>   <u>percents</u>

Step 3: $\dfrac{\$600}{\$n} = \dfrac{15}{100}$

Step 4:   Cross multiply: $15 \times n = 600 \times 100$

$$15n = 60,000$$

Divide: $n = \dfrac{60,000}{15} = \mathbf{\$4,000}$

Example 5:   What is 40% of 65?

Step 1:   *question:* What is?
You are looking for the part.

Step 2:   *necessary information:* 40%, of 65
40% is the percent.
65 is the whole.

Step 3:   Set up a proportion in this form:

<u>numbers</u> <u>percents</u>

$$\frac{n}{65} = \frac{40}{100}$$

Step 4:   Cross multiply: $100 \times n = 65 \times 40$

$$100n = 2{,}600$$

Divide: $n = \frac{2{,}600}{100} = \mathbf{26}$

Example 6:   June decided that she could spend 25% of her income for rent. She makes $580 a month. How much can she spend for rent?

Step 1:   *question:* How much can she spend for rent?
We are looking for the part of her income that she will spend on rent.

Step 2:   *necessary information:* 25%, $580
25% is the percent.
$580 is her whole income.

Step 3:   *proportion:*

<u>numbers</u>   <u>percents</u>

$$\frac{\$n}{\$580} = \frac{25}{100}$$

Step 4:   Cross multiply: $100 \times n = 580 \times 25$

$$100n = 14{,}500$$

Divide: $n = \frac{14{,}500}{100} = \mathbf{\$145}$

EXERCISE 2:   Solve the following problems by using proportions.

1.   36 is what % of 144?

_____

2.   288 is 72% of what number?

_____

3. What is 68% of 75?

    _____

4. A $160 suit was reduced by $40. What was the
    percent of the reduction?

    _____

5. Marsha received 58% of the vote when she ran
    for the school board. 28,450 votes were cast.
    How many votes did she receive?

    _____

6. The state government cut aid for adult education
    by 25%. Metropolis expects to lose $96,000. How
    much aid for adult education had Metropolis
    been receiving?

    _____

7. Last year Jeffrey paid 7% of his income in taxes.
    He paid $553. What was his income?

    _____

8. 60% of the residents of the city are black. The
    population of the city is 345,780. How many
    black people live in the city?

    _____

9. In 1982, Robyn paid $340 interest on $2,000 that
    she had borrowed. What was the interest rate on
    the borrowed money?

    _____

Answers on page 160.

SOLVING PERCENT WORD PROBLEMS
INVOLVING DECIMALS AND FRACTIONS

Many percent word problems also contain decimals or fractions. These problems are also solved using the proportion method.

Example 1: What is $33\frac{1}{3}\%$ of 54?

   Step 1: *question:* What is?
You are looking for the part.

   Step 2: *necessary information:* $33\frac{1}{3}\%$, of 54

$33\frac{1}{3}\%$ is the percent.

54 is the whole.

   Step 3: *proportion:*

$$\frac{n}{54} = \frac{33\frac{1}{3}}{100}$$

   Step 4: Cross multiply and divide:

$100 \times n = 33\frac{1}{3} \times 54$

$100n = 1{,}800$

$n = \frac{1{,}800}{100} = \mathbf{18}$

Example 2: Bob takes home \$156.40 out of his weekly pay of \$184. What percent of his pay does he take home?

   Step 1: *question:* What percent of his pay does he take home?
You are looking for the percent.

   Step 2: *necessary information:* \$156.40, \$184

\$156.40 is the part.

\$184 is the whole.

   Step 3: *proportion:*

$$\frac{\$156.40}{\$184} = \frac{n}{100}$$

   Step 4: Cross multiply and divide:

$184 \times n = 156.40 \times 100$

$184n = 15{,}640$

$n = \frac{15{,}640}{184} = \mathbf{85\%}$

EXERCISE 3: Solve the following percent problems using proportions.

    1. 4.5% of what number is 90?

2. $\frac{1}{10}$ is what percent of $\frac{3}{4}$?

_____

3. $66\frac{2}{3}\%$ of what number is 42?

_____

4. What is 6.4% of 800?

_____

5. Russo's Restaurant collected $49.76 in taxes Friday night. The food tax is 8%. How much money did the restaurant receive for meals on Friday night?

_____

6. Jed bought a steak dinner for $8.60. He paid a 5% tax on it. How much was the tax?

_____

7. Glenda bought maple syrup for $1.92 a pint and sold the syrup for $.96 a pint more. By what percent did she mark up the price of the maple syrup?

_____

8. Barnes and Noble was having a store-wide book-sale in which all prices were cut $12\frac{1}{2}\%$. How much did Juan save on a book that normally costs $12.80?

_____

Answers on page 160.

PERCENT WORD PROBLEM REVIEW

The following problems give you a chance to review percent word problems containing whole numbers, decimals and fractions.

EXERCISE 4.   Solve the problems by using proportions.

1. 3 out of 4 dentists recommend a fluoride tooth-paste. What percent of all dentists recommend a fluoride toothpaste?

_____

2. 112,492 people voted for mayor in the city. This was 40% of the registered voters. How many registered voters are there in the city?

_____

3. In a normal season, the Seaside Resort has 34,500 visitors. This year, due to bad weather, 11,500 fewer visitors came to the resort. What was the percent drop in business for the resort?

_____

4. The High Tech Electronics Company announced an 8.6% profit on sales of $49,600,000. How much profit did the company make?

_____

5. The Quality Chocolate Company decided to increase the size of its chocolate bar .4 ounce. This was an increase in size of $16\frac{2}{3}\%$. What was the weight of its chocolate bar before the change?

_____

6. In a recent flu epidemic, .8% of people over age 65 who caught the disease died. The death toll in this group was 40. How many people over age 65 caught the flu?

   _____

7. Last year Dennis paid 13% of his income in taxes. He earned $11,694. How much did he pay in income taxes?

   _____

8. The Machinist's Union has just won a 7% raise for its members. Dan is a union member who was making $17,548. How much of a raise will he get?

   _____

9. Nayana received a 9% raise worth $18 a week. What had her week's salary been?

   _____

10. Basketball star Kareem scored on 506 out of 1,012 attempts. What was his scoring percentage?

    _____

Answers on page 161.

CHAPTER 10:
Combination Word Problems

SOLVING COMBINATION WORD PROBLEMS

Until now, this book has shown you one-step word problems. However, many situations require that you use a combination of math operations to solve word problems.

Generally, you can solve these combination problems by breaking them into two or more one-step problems. As you read a word problem, you may see that it will take more than one math operation to solve. The difficulty lies in deciding how many steps to take and in what order to work them out.

The key to solving combination problems is:

Start with the question and work backwards.

This shouldn't be difficult. Throughout this book, you have started your work with finding the question.

The steps in solving combination word problems:

> **Step 1:** Find the question.
> **Step 2:** Select the necessary information.
> **Step 3:** Write a solution sentence for the problem. Fill in only the necessary information that belongs in the solution sentence.
> Write another sentence, this time to find the information that is missing in the solution sentence. Solve the sentence that gives you the missing information.
> **Step 4:** Fill in the missing information (the answer from Step 3) in the solution sentence and solve.
> **Step 5:** Make sure that the answer is sensible.

No matter how many short problems a combination problem consists of, you can always work backwards from the solution sentence. Examples 1 and 2 illustrate this.

Example 1: Sengchen had $38 in her checking account. She wrote checks for $14 and $9. How much money was left in her checking account?

  Step 1: *question:* How much money was left in her checking account?

  Step 2: *necessary information:* $38, $14, $9

Step 3:	Write a solution sentence.	

Step 3: Write a solution sentence.
money − checks = money left
Fill in the sentence with information that can be used to solve the problem.
Decide what *missing information* is needed to solve the problem. Write a number sentence and solve.
check + check = checks
$14 + $9 = $23
Now you have the complete information needed to solve the problem.

$38 − *checks* = money left

$38 − $23 = money left

Step 4: Solve.

$38 − $23 = **$15 left**

Example 2: Lillie worked as a travel agent. How much money did she collect from a group that traveled to Las Vegas? 56 people went on the trip at an individual cost of $165 in airfare plus $230 hotel accommodations.

Step 1: *question:* How much money did she collect?

Step 2: *necessary information:* 56 people, $165 airfare, $230 hotel accommodations

Step 3: Write a solution sentence:
cost × number of people = total
solve for *missing information:*
airfare + hotel = cost
$165 + $230 = $395

cost × 56 = total cost

$395 × 56 = total cost

Step 4: Solve.

$395 × 56 = **$22,120 total**

The words that you use in the solution and missing information sentences may differ from what we have here. What is important is that you break down the problem into smaller steps.

A combination word problem that needs both multiplication and division to be solved can often be written as one proportion instead of two separate word sentences. If you need to review writing and solving proportions, see Chapter 7: Using Proportions: Multiplication, Division, and Conversion Word Problems.

Example 3: Apples were sold at a cost of 2 pounds for 58 cents. How much did Michelle pay for 3 pounds of apples?

Step 1: *question:* How much did Michelle pay for 3 pounds of apples?

Step 2: *necessary information:* 2 pounds, 58 cents, 3 pounds

Step 3: Write a proportion to show the relationship between weight and cost.

Step 4: Fill in the appropriate numbers and solve.

$$\frac{pounds}{cents} = \frac{pounds}{cents}$$

$$\frac{2 \text{ pounds}}{58 \text{ cents}} = \frac{3 \text{ pounds}}{n}$$

$$2 \times n = 3 \times 58$$

$$n = \frac{174}{2} = \textbf{87 cents}$$

After some practice, you will be able to tell which problems can be solved with a proportion. In most cases, breaking down a problem into smaller problems with word sentences will be the best method for solution.

EXERCISE 1:   For each word problem, write two word sentences (a solution sentence and a missing information sentence) or a proportion. DO NOT SOLVE!!

1. Tim earns $230 dollars a week. Every week, $49 in taxes and $6 in union dues are taken out of his paycheck. What is his take-home pay?

   _____

   _____

2. After starting the day with $41 dollars, Miguel spent $3 for lunch and $22 for gas. How much money did he have left by the end of the day?

   _____

   _____

3. Samuel had $394 in his checking account. After writing a check for $187 and depositing $201, how much money was in his checking account?

   _____

   _____

4. Kelly bought 5 blouses for $12 each and a skirt for $16. How much money did she spend on these clothes?

   _____

   _____

5. Martha borrowed $4,600 to buy a new car. She will have to pay $728 interest. She plans to pay back the loan plus the interest in 24 equal monthly payments. How much will her monthly payments be?

   _____

   _____

6. A store bought 30 boxes of dolls for $720. If there were 8 dolls in a box, how much did each doll cost?

_____

_____

7. At the candy counter, licorice cost 5 cents for 3 pieces. Cindy gave her daughter Emily 30 cents to spend on licorice. How many pieces of licorice was Emily able to buy?

_____

_____

8. Jocelyn bought a skirt for $14 and a blouse for $9. She paid for the clothes with a $100 bill. What was her change?

_____

_____

9. In order to be hired, a data entry operator must be able to enter numbers into a computer at the rate of 10,000 numbers every 60 minutes. Yvana took a 15 minute data entry test. How many numbers did she have to enter in order to be hired?

_____

_____

10. A school needs to determine how many square feet of carpet to order for three rooms. If each room measures 20 feet long by 15 feet wide, how many square feet of carpeting must be ordered?

_____

_____

Answers on page 162.

EXERCISE 2:   Write the two one-step word sentences or the proportion needed to solve the following combination word problems. Then solve the problems.

1. For the convention, each of the 8 wards of the city elected 4 delegates, while 5 delegates were elected at large. How many delegates did the city send to the convention?

——————————

2. It cost the gas station owner $81 in parts and $45 in labor to fix his customer's car. He charged his customer $163. How much profit did the owner make on the job?

——————————

3. After working at the copying machine for 5 minutes, Angie had made 30 copies. If she continued working at the same rate, how many copies would she make in an hour (60 minutes)?

——————————

4. 4 friends evenly split the $216 it cost to drive a car to Florida. Jennifer then spent $114 on her own for the rest of her vacation. How much did Jennifer spend on her vacation?

——————————

5. The AFL-CIO chartered buses to go to a demonstration in Washington. 4,168 union members and 1,272 other people signed up for the buses. How many buses did they have to charter, if they could fit 40 people on a bus?

_____

6. Mark was offered a job downtown that would give him a raise of $78 a month over his current salary, but his commuting costs would be $2 a day higher. If he works 22 days a month, what would be his net monthly increase in pay?

_____

7. A recipe for 6 people calls for 3 pounds of stew beef. Ginny is planning to make the recipe for 8 people. How much stew beef does she need?

_____

8. On election day, 7,481 ballots were cast at town hall. The election officials counted 4,201 votes for Ronald Reagan and 2,896 votes for Jimmy Carter. How many ballots were cast for a candidate other than Reagan or Carter?

_____

Answers on page 163.

SOLVING COMBINATION WORD PROBLEMS:
DECIMALS, FRACTIONS, PERCENTS

Decimal, fraction, and percent combination word problems are set up and solved in the same way as whole number combination word problems.

Example 1:   For each child at her daughter's birthday party, Shelly spent $.35 for a party favor and $.16 for a balloon. She had 13 children at the party. How much did she spend for gifts for the children?

Step 1:   *question:*   How much did she spend for gifts for the children?

Step 2:   *necessary information:* $.35, $.16, 13 children

Step 3:   *solution sentence:*

gifts × children = total cost   *gifts* × 13 = total cost

missing information sentence:
favor + balloon = gifts
$.35 + $.16 = $.51   *$.51* × 13 = total cost

Step 4:   Solve.   *$.51* × 13 = **$6.63**

Example 2:   Bright's department store advertised that everything in the store was $\frac{1}{5}$ off. Debbie bought a pair of pants labeled $20. How much did the pants cost her?

Step 1:   *question:*   How much did the pants cost her?

Step 2:   *necessary information:* $\frac{1}{5}$, $20

Step 3:   *solution sentence:*

original price − discount = sale price $20 − *discount* = sale pr

missing information sentence:
price × fraction = discount
$20 × $\frac{1}{5}$ = $4 discount $20 − $4 = sale price

Step 4:   Solve. $20 − $4 = **$16**

Both of these examples illustrate two-step word problems. Later in this chapter you will work with problems that need more than two steps for solution.

Example 3:   Real Value Hardware advertised that all prices had been reduced 15%. A socket set is on sale for $13.60. What was its original price?

Step 1:   *question:* What was its original price?

Step 2:   *necessary information:* 15%, $13.60

Step 3:   *solution statement:* Since this is a percent problem you can write a proportion.

$$\frac{\text{part}}{\text{whole}} = \frac{\text{percent}}{100} \qquad\qquad \frac{13.60}{n} = \frac{percent}{100}$$

missing information:
100% − percent reduced = percent sale
100% − 15% = 85%

$$\frac{13.60}{n} = \frac{85}{100}$$

Step 4:   Solve.

$$85 \times n = 13.60 \times 100$$
$$85n = 1{,}360$$
$$n = \$16$$

EXERCISE 3:   Write in words the two one-step word sentences or the proportion needed to solve the combination word problem. Then solve the problem.

1.   Chris bought 6 boxes of cookies for $14.40. If there were 20 cookies in a box, how much did each cookie cost?

   _____

2.   A $400 washing machine was reduced 30% for clearance. What was its sale price?

   _____

3.   Beverley bought 5 cans of pears, each containing $9\frac{3}{4}$ ounces of pears and 1 can of fruit cocktail containing $17\frac{1}{2}$ ounces of fruit. What was the total weight of the fruit she bought?

   _____

4. A water widget cost Phil $2.49. Because it reduced his use of hot water, it saved him $3.40 a month in costs for hot water. What was his net savings for 12 months?

_____

5. When cooked, a hamburger loses $\frac{1}{3}$ of its original weight. How much does a $\frac{1}{4}$-pound hamburger weigh after it is cooked?

_____

6. The tax on a meal is 6%. How much is Milton's total bill on a $24.00 dinner?

_____

7. During the summer clearance sale, everything in the store was 30% off. Solaire bought a bathing suit that normally sells for $19.50. How much did she pay for the suit?

_____

8. Marlene bought a new couch for $310.60. She paid $130 down and planned to pay the rest in 12 equal monthly payments. How much will she pay each month?

_____

9. Walter bought a case of 30 bottles of cooking oil for $57. He then sold the oil for $2.10 per bottle. How much money did he make on each bottle?

_____

10. Walter bought a case of 30 bottles of cooking oil for $57. He then sold the oil for a profit of $.20 per bottle. What was the percent of profit? (Round to the nearest tenth of a percent.)

_____

Answers on page 164.

SOLVING COMBINATION WORD PROBLEMS INVOLVING CONVERSIONS

Many combination word problems involve conversions. To solve the following examples and problems, you should refer to the conversion chart on page 87. You should notice that a conversion is needed when one unit of measurement appears in the necessary information and a different unit of measurement is called for in the question.

Example 1: A dairy farm sold 156 quarts of milk at its own store and shipped out an additional 868 quarts to nearby supermarkets. How many gallons of milk were marketed?

Step 1: *question:* How many gallons of milk were marketed?

Step 2: *necessary information:* 156 quarts, 868 quarts

Step 3: *solution statement:*

$$\frac{quarts}{gallon} = \frac{quarts}{gallon} \qquad \frac{4}{1} = \frac{quarts}{n\ gallons}$$

There are four quarts in a gallon. This is written on the left side of the proportion as $\frac{4}{1}$.

missing information sentence:
quarts + quarts = total quarts
156 + 868 = 1,024 quarts

$$\frac{4}{1} = \frac{1,024}{n}$$

Step 4: Solve.

$$4 \times n = 1 \times 1,024$$
$$4n = 1,024$$
$$n = \frac{1,024}{4} = 256\ \textbf{gallons}$$

Example 2:   A mill is cutting 8-<u>foot</u> lengths of lumber into chair legs. There are 6 <u>inches</u> of scrap for each length. What percent of the wood is scrap?

Step 1:   *question:* What percent of the wood is scrap?

Step 2:   *necessary information:* 8 foot, 6 inches

Step 3:   *solution statement:*

$$\frac{part}{whole} = \frac{percent}{100} \qquad\qquad \frac{6 \text{ inches}}{8 \text{ feet}} = \frac{n}{100}$$

Since all the information must be in the same unit of measurement, do the conversion.

conversion:
$$\frac{1 \text{ foot}}{12 \text{ inches}} = \frac{8 \text{ feet}}{x}$$
$$x = 12 \times 8$$
$$x = 96 \text{ inches}$$

Note: In the conversion, the letter x was used to stand for the unknown number of inches. Any letter can be used to stand for an unknown.

Step 4:   Solve.

$$\frac{6 \text{ inches}}{96 \text{ inches}} = \frac{n}{100}$$
$$96 \times n = 6 \times 100$$
$$96n = 600$$
$$n = \frac{600}{96} = 6\frac{1}{4}\%$$

EXERCISE 4:   Solve the following word problems, making the necessary conversions. Be careful; not all problems need a conversion.

1. Tile Town sells 81-square-inch tiles. How many tiles are needed to cover a 54-square-foot floor?

_____

2. On the airplane assembly line, Isadore was able to make 20 welds an hour. How may welds did he make during a 9-hour work day?

_____

3. On a 46-mile stretch of Interstate Highway, there is a reflector every 528 feet. How many reflectors are there on the stretch of highway?

_____

4. The medical center needed 48 gallons of blood after the earthquake. A nearby city donated 26 gallons of blood. The rest was donated at the medical center by people each giving one pint of blood. How many people gave a pint of blood at the center?

_____

5. The Heat Coal Company distributed 38 tons of coal in one day to its customers. It delivered 400 pounds of coal to each of its customers. How many customers received deliveries?

_____

6 Sharon was able to type 463 numbers during a 5-minute timing for data entry. At this rate, how many numbers could she type in an hour?

_____

7. Lynn brought 12 quarts of ice cream to the Fourth of July picnic. If she gives each person a 4-ounce serving of ice cream, how many people will get the ice cream?

_____

Answers on page 165.

SOLVING WORD PROBLEMS
CONTAINING UNNECESSARY INFORMATION

Throughout the exercises in this book, you have seen problems that contain unnecessary information. These numbers are more difficult to spot in combination word problems than in one-step word problems. The key to identifying numbers as unnecessary is in working backwards from the question as you have been doing. Once you write a word sentence that will answer the question, look at all the given information and decide what is needed to answer the question.

Example 1: At sunrise, the temperature was 54 degrees. By mid-afternoon it had risen 27 degrees. The temperature then began falling, until by midnight it had dropped 19 degrees from the high. What was the temperature at mid-afternoon?

Step 1: *question:* What was the temperature at mid-afternoon?

Step 2: *necessary information:* 54 degrees, 27 degrees (The fact that the temperature had dropped another 19 degrees by midnight is not necessary information.)

Step 3: This is a one-step problem. Write a word sentence: sunrise temperature + change = mid-afternoon temperature

Step 4: Solve:
54 + 27 = **81 degrees**

Example 2: An .8-ounce jar of basil sells for $.98. Marie plans to pack 3.5 pounds of basil into the jars. How many jars will she need?

Step 1: *question:* How many jars will she need?

Step 2: *necessary information:* .8 ounce, 3.5 pounds
(The cost of the jar of basil is not necessary information.)

Step 3: *solution proportion:*

$$\frac{\text{total weight}}{\text{number of jars}} = \frac{\text{weight}}{1 \text{ jar}} \qquad \frac{3.5 \text{ pounds}}{n \text{ jars}} = \frac{.8 \text{ ounce}}{1 \text{ jar}}$$

Since all your weights must be in the same unit of measurement, your next step must be a conversion to find the number of ounces in a pound.

conversion:
$$\frac{16 \text{ ounces}}{1 \text{ pound}} = \frac{n \text{ ounces}}{3.5 \text{ pounds}}$$

$$1 \times n = 3.5 \times 16$$
$$n = 56 \text{ ounces}$$

$$\frac{56 \text{ ounces}}{n \text{ jars}} = \frac{.8 \text{ ounce}}{1 \text{ jar}}$$
$$.8 \times n = 56 \times 1$$

Step 4: Solve.

$$.8n = 56$$

$$n = \frac{56}{.8} = 70 \text{ jars}$$

EXERCISE 5: Write the word sentences or proportion needed to solve the following word problems. Underline the necessary information. Then solve the problem. Be careful; many of these problems contain unnecessary information.

1. At the beginning of the school year, the Philadelphia school system had 103,912 students. During the course of the year 4,657 students left the system while 1,288 more students were enrolled. What was the student population at the end of the year?

   _____

2. At the beginning of the school year, the Philadelphia school system had 103,912 students. During the course of the year 4,657 students left the system while 1,288 more students were enrolled. How many different students spent at least part of the year in the Philadelphia school system?

   _____

3. At sunrise, the temperature was 54 degrees. By mid-afternoon it had risen 27 degrees. The temperature then began falling, until by midnight it had dropped 19 degrees from the high. What was the temperature at midnight?

   _____

4. Every week, after having $53 taken out of his pay-check, Lloyd brings home $148. What was Lloyd's total take-home pay for a 52-week year?

_____

5. Ahmed bought 3 paperbacks for $2.95 each at the bookstore, and 2 magazines for $1.50 each at the drugstore. He paid for his books with a 10-dollar bill. How much change did he receive at the bookstore?

_____

6. Sangita is a member of a cooperative grocery store. She gets a 20% discount on everything she buys in the store. She bought a 5-pound bag of oranges marked $1.65. After receiving her discount, how much did she pay for the oranges?

_____

Answers on page 165.

SOLVING LONGER COMBINATION WORD PROBLEMS

Sometimes word problems cannot be solved by being broken into two one-step problems. Three or more steps may be needed to solve the problem. The method used with these problems is the same as the method used throughout this chapter with combination word problems. Keep working backwards from the question. Set up a solution sentence and solve shorter problems to get all of the information that you need.

Example: Sylvia went shopping in the bargain basement. She bought a $24.99 dress marked $\frac{1}{3}$ off and a $16.95 pair of pants marked down 20%. How much did she spend?

Step 1:   *question:* How much did she spend?

Step 2:   *necessary information:* $24.99, $\frac{1}{3}$ off; $16.95, 20% marked down

Step 3:   *solution sentence:*

dress price + *pants price* = total spent

In order to solve this you must find the sale prices of both the dress and the pants. Both can be found by using this *missing information* sentence:

original price − *discount amount* = *sale price*

You can find the discount by multiplying the original amount by a fraction or percent.

dress

$24.99 − ($\frac{1}{3}$ × 24.99) = *sale price*

24.99 − 8.33 = $16.66

pants

$16.95 − (20% of 16.95) = *sale price*

16.95 − (.20 × 16.95) = *sale price*

16.95 − 3.39 = $13.56

Step 4:   Solve.

$16.66 + $13.56 = **$30.22**

Note: Chapter 9 used the proportion method for solving percent word problems. However, if a problem requires you to find a percent of an amount there is another method. Simply change the percent to a decimal and multiply. In the example above 20% was changed to .20.

EXERCISE 6:   For every problem, write all necessary word sentences or proportions. Then solve the problem. Round off all money solutions to the nearest penny.

1. Apples cost $1.56 a dozen. Kerry bought 7 apples in addition to buying a cantaloupe for $.88. How much did she spend?

2. Aaron received a gas bill of $36.80 for 32 gallons of bottled gas. If he pays the bill within 10 days, he will receive a 6% discount. How much will he have to pay if he pays his bill within 10 days?

    _____

3. Harold's doctor advised him to cut down on the calories he consumed by 28%. Harold had been consuming 4,200 calories a day. If Harold's breakfast contains 797 calories, how many calories can he have during the rest of the day?

    _____

4. Sarkis is a salesman. He receives a salary of $70 a week plus a 6% commission on all his sales over $200. Last week, he sold $1,160 worth of merchandise. What was he paid for the week?

    _____

5. Dinora drove 3,627 miles from coast to coast. Her car averaged 31 miles per gallon, and she spent $186 for gas. On the average, what did she pay per gallon of gas?

    _____

Answers on page 166.

REVIEW: SOLVING COMBINATION WORD PROBLEMS

EXERCISE 7:   For all problems, choose the one best answer. Round off decimals to the nearest penny or the nearest hundredth.

1. Every day Kevin has to drive 7 miles each way to work and back. At work he has to drive his truck on a 296-mile delivery route. How many miles does he drive during a 5-day work week?

    a. *310 miles*
    b. *315 miles*
    c. *1,550 miles*
    d. *4,214 miles*
    e. *none of the above*

2. Every day Jason has a 14-mile round trip drive to work. He then has to drive his truck on a 296-mile delivery route 5 days a week. How many miles does he drive each day?

    a. *310 miles*
    b. *315 miles*
    c. *1,550 miles*
    d. *4,214 miles*
    e. *none of the above*

3. For his art class, Karl spent $135 on books and $225 on materials. In order to cover costs, how much did each of his 15 students have to pay?

    a. *$360*
    b. *$90*
    c. *$24*
    d. *$15*
    e. *$9*

4. Jessie's restaurant had 4 small dining rooms with a capacity of 28 people each, and a main dining room with a capacity of 94 people. What was the total capacity of the restaurant?

    a. *126 people*
    b. *658 people*
    c. *348 people*
    d. *122 people*
    e. *206 people*

5. Each team in the 8-team football league used to have a roster of 36 players. The league decided to decrease each team's roster size by 3 players. Before the change, how many players were in the league?

a. *180 players*
b. *288 players*
c. *285 players*
d. *264 players*
e. *396 players*

6. Each team in the 8-team football league used to have a roster of 36 players. The league decided to decrease each team's roster size by 3 players. After the change, how many players were in the league?

a. *180 players*
b. *288 players*
c. *285 players*
d. *264 players*
e. *396 players*

7. At the supermarket, Monique bought 2.36 pounds of cheese and 4 pounds of apples. The apples cost $.49 per pound and the cheese cost $1.58 per pound. What was the total cost of the cheese and apples?

a. *$7.48*
b. *$4.43*
c. *$3.94*
d. *$5.69*
e. *$4.29*

8. A bottle contains 6 cups of laundry detergent. The directions say to use $\frac{1}{3}$ cup for a top loading washer and $\frac{1}{4}$ cup for a front loading washer. How many more loads per bottle can you do with a front loading washer than with a top loading washer?

a. *1 load*
b. *3 loads*
c. *6 loads*
d. *8 loads*
e. *9 loads*

9. Nora pays her babysitter an average of $90 a week. How much does she pay her babysitter in a year?

   a. *$1,080*
   b. *$4,680*
   c. *$142*
   d. *$5,400*
   e. *none of the above*

10. A factory worker packed 12 pencils in a package and 60 packages in a box. He sent out 17 boxes of pencils. How many pencils did he send out?

    a. *720 pencils*
    b. *85 pencils*
    c. *89 pencils*
    d. *1,740 pencils*
    e. *12,240 pencils*

Answers on page 166.

CHAPTER 11:
Word Problem Review

For all problems, choose the best answer.

1. 3 tablespoons cocoa plus 1 tablespoon fat can be substituted for 1 ounce chocolate in baking recipes. A recipe for chocolate cake calls for 12 ounces of chocolate. If Shirley is substituting cocoa for chocolate, how much cocoa should she use?

   a. *15 tablespoons*
   b. *9 tablespoons*
   c. *4 tablespoons*
   d. *36 tablespoons*
   e. *17 tablespoons*

2. 1 cup sugar plus $\frac{1}{4}$ cup liquid can be substituted for 1 cup corn syrup in baking recipes. A recipe calls for $1\frac{1}{2}$ cups corn syrup. If Mira is substituting sugar for corn syrup, how much liquid should she add?

   a. $\frac{3}{8}$ *cup*
   b. $\frac{1}{6}$ *cup*
   c. *6 cups*
   d. $1\frac{1}{4}$ *cups*
   e. $3\frac{3}{4}$ *cups*

3. Matt has a 400-square-inch board. He needs a 25-square-inch piece of the board for the floor of a birdhouse. What percent of the board will he need for the birdhouse?

   a. *425 square inches*
   b. *375 square inches*
   c. $6\frac{1}{4}\%$
   d. $93\frac{3}{4}\%$
   e. *100%*

4. A bushel of apples weighs 48 pounds. Tanya wants to buy 12 pounds of apples. How many bushels should she buy?

   a. *4 bushels*
   b. *36 bushels*
   c. $\frac{1}{2}$ *bushel*
   d. $\frac{1}{4}$ *bushel*
   e. *none of the above*

5. 1.23 cubic yards of concrete are needed to cover 100 square feet with 4 inches of concrete. How many cubic yards are needed to cover 550 square feet with 4 inches of concrete?

   a. *650 square feet*
   b. *4.92 cubic yards*
   c. *6.765 cubic yards*
   d. *2,200 square inches*
   e. *27.06 cubic yards*

6. Large eggs weigh $1\frac{1}{2}$ pounds per dozen. Dawn bought 8 large eggs. How much did the eggs weigh?

   a. *3 ounces*
   b. *$\frac{1}{3}$ pound*
   c. *1 pound*
   d. *18 ounces*
   e. *none of the above*

7. Melvin received an electric bill for $86.29. He knows that it cost him $59 a month for his air conditioning. How much would his bill have been if he had not operated the air conditioner?

   a. *$155.29*
   b. *$27.29*
   c. *$50.91*
   d. *$14.63*
   e. *none of the above*

8. If Kenneth retires at age 65, he will receive as a pension 80% of his salary of $18,657. If he retires at age 62, he will receive only 70% of his salary. How much smaller will his pension be if he retires early?

   a. *$1,865.70*
   b. *$10*
   c. *$18,507*
   d. *$3,331.41*
   e. *$13,059.90*

9. An oil truck carried 9,008 gallons of oil. After making 7 deliveries averaging 364 gallons each, how much oil was left in the truck?

   a. *174 gallons*
   b. *9,379 gallons*
   c. *8,644 gallons*
   d. *6,460 gallons*
   e. *8,637 gallons*

10. A conservation organization charged each member $10 dues plus $5 for their magazine. How much money did the organization collect from its 13,819 members?

   a. $207,285
   b. $138,190
   c. $69,095
   d. $690,950
   e. $138,195

11. For her wardrobe, Mrs. Are was given a Paris original worth $1,343, a New York original worth $658, and a Goodwill original worth $3.98. What was the total value of the clothes given to her?

   a. $2,004.98
   b. $668
   c. $1,997.02
   d. $681.02
   e. $1,346.98

12. After 3 years, Elsie's car had lost $\frac{1}{3}$ of its original value. Two years later, it had lost an additional $\frac{1}{4}$ of its original value. If she bought the car for $3,600, what was it worth after the five years?

   a. $4,800
   b. $2,700
   c. $3,300
   d $2,100
   e. $1,500

13. Glenn, the owner of a hardware store, originally paid $540.60 for 15 tool sets. At his year-end clearance sale, he sold the last tool set for $24. How much money did he lose on the last tool set?

   a. $180.60
   b. $1.50
   c. $12.04
   d. $36.04
   e. *none of the above*

14. After having $48.23 taken out of his paycheck, Maurice takes home $132.77 every week. What are Maurice's total gross earnings for a 52-week year?

    a. *$4,396.08*
    b. *$9,412*
    c. *$8,814.90*
    d. *$6,904.04*
    e. *$2,507.96*

15. Peter's allergy pills come in a 250-tablet bottle. He takes 4 tablets a day. How many tablets did he have left after taking the tablets for 30 days?

    a. *130 tablets*
    b. *216 tablets*
    c. *120 tablets*
    d. *370 tablets*
    e. *none of the above*

16. Money available for financial aid at Santa Clara Community College has dropped $462,000 from last year's $1,126,200. The college decided to divide the aid evenly among 820 students who needed the money. How much did each student get in financial aid?

    a. *$563.41*
    b. *$810*
    c. *$1,373.41*
    d. *$1,936.82*
    e. *none of the above*

17. Nickilena, Jean, Rosemary, and Elaine went into business together. The 4-woman partnership earned $36,460 and had expenses of $23,188. If they split the profits evenly, how much did each woman make?

    a. *$5,797*
    b. *$3,318*
    c. *$14,912*
    d. *$9,115*
    e. *$14,073*

18. After driving 168 miles, Tony needed 5.6 gallons of gasoline to fill his gas tank. How many gallons of gasoline would he use for the 417-mile drive from his home in Los Angeles to his brother's home near San Francisco?

a. *44.5 gallons*
b. *13.9 gallons*
c. *74.5 gallons*
d. *8.3 gallons*
e. *19.5 gallons*

19. Diana makes lemonade from the powdered concentrate by combining 5 tablespoons of concentrate with 2 cups of water. The directions say you should use 24 cups of water for the entire container of concentrate. How many tablespoons of concentrate are in the container?

a. *240 tablespoons*
b. *130 tablespoons*
c. *110 tablespoons*
d. *60 tablespoons*
e. *31 tablespoons*

20. A pile of books weighed 34.2 pounds. If each book weighed .6 pound, how many books were in the pile?

a. *35 books*
b. *34 books*
c. *21 books*
d. *20 books*
e. *57 books*

21. There are 5,372 school age children in town. 1,547 either go to private school or have dropped out. How many children remain in the town's public schools?

a. *6,919 children*
b. *3,825 children*
c. *4,235 children*
d. *4,839 children*
e. *none of the above*

22. 423 service stations in the state closed in the last year. Only 2,135 remain. How many service stations were there in the state a year ago?

   a. *2,558 service stations*
   b. *1,712 service stations*
   c. *2,312 service stations*
   d. *2,512 service stations*
   e. *none of the above*

23. There are 3 feet in a yard. There are 1,760 yards in a mile. How many feet are there in a 5 mile race?

   a. *15 feet*
   b. *$2,935\frac{2}{3}$ feet*
   c. *26,400 feet*
   d. *8,800 feet*
   e. *5,280 feet*

24. Manny was working as a hot dog vendor. He sold a total of 426 hot dogs in one weekend. If he sold 198 on Saturday, how many did he sell on Sunday?

   a. *624 hot dogs*
   b. *332 hot dogs*
   c. *228 hot dogs*
   d. *514 hot dogs*
   e. *none of the above*

25. During the Washington's Birthday Clearance Sale, Gayle bought a $96 winter coat that was reduced by $\frac{1}{3}$. What was the sale price of the coat?

   a. *$32*
   b. *$64*
   c. *$288*
   d. *$93*
   e. *none of the above*

26. During the sale, Naisuon bought a three-piece wool suit that was reduced by $47 to $95. What was the original price of the suit?

   a. *$48*
   b. *$52*
   c. *$132*
   d. *$142*
   e. *none of the above*

27. Naomi had $61 in her checking account. She wrote a check for $28 and made a $115 deposit. How much money did she then have in the account?

    a. *$204*
    b. *$24*
    c. *$148*
    d *$82*
    e. *$34*

28. Maureen weighed $172\frac{1}{2}$ pounds. She lost $47\frac{3}{4}$ pounds in one year. What was her new weight?

    a. *$219\frac{1}{4}$ pounds*
    b. *$118\frac{3}{4}$ pounds*
    c. *$124\frac{3}{4}$ pounds*
    d. *$125\frac{1}{4}$ pounds*
    e. *none of the above*

29. Carla gained 3 pounds in the first month of her new diet and 4 pounds in the second month. Her original weight was 104 pounds. What was her new weight?

    a. *97 pounds*
    b. *105 pounds*
    c. *103 pounds*
    d. *111 pounds*
    e. *100 pounds*

30. Out of 1,400 people polled, 68% were in favor of a nuclear arms freeze and 25% were against it. How many people were undecided?

    a. *93 people*
    b. *350 people*
    c. *952 people*
    d. *98 people*
    e. *1,307 people*

31. Glennie had $74.81 in her checking account. She wrote checks for $46.19 and $22.45. She then made a $60.00 deposit. What was her new balance?

    a. *$203.45*
    b. *$66.17*
    c. *$83.45*
    d. *$53.83*
    e. *$38.55*

32. Eileen bought 3 pairs of socks for $1.79 each and 4 towels for $2.69 each. How much did she spend?

    a. *$4.48*
    b. *$11.48*
    c. *$31.36*
    d. *$16.13*
    e. *$7.00*

33. After paying $14.43 for dinner and $3.50 for a movie, Florence paid the babysitter $5. How much did the evening cost her?

    a. *$12.93*
    b. *$22.93*
    c. *$5.93*
    d. *$8.50*
    e. *$19.43*

34. On the average, Kennedy Airport has 96 jumbo jets arriving each day. Each jumbo jet has an average of 214 passengers. How many passengers arrive by jumbo jet at Kennedy Airport each day?

    a. *310 passengers*
    b. *20,544 passengers*
    c. *118 passengers*
    d. *222 passengers*
    e. *none of the above*

35. The list price of an automobile was $6,578. Jane ordered $435 of added options and received a $650 rebate. How much did Jane pay for the car?

    a. *$7,663*
    b. *$7,013*
    c. *$7,228*
    d. *$5,493*
    e. *$6,363*

36. In the first quarter, the Philadelphia 76ers missed only 7 out of 25 field goal attempts. What was their scoring percentage?

    a. *72%*
    b. *76%*
    c. *28%*
    d. *32%*
    e. *18%*

37. 28% of the workers at the factory were women. There were 432 male workers. What was the total number of workers at the factory?

a. *460 workers*
b. *12,096 workers*
c. *600 workers*
d. *1,543 workers*
e. *404 workers*

38. 1,600 pounds of steel are used to make a Chevrolet. The automobile plant produced 840 Chevrolets in one day. How many pounds of steel were needed that day to make the cars?

a. *2,440 pounds*
b. *1,344,000 pounds*
c. *760 pounds*
d. *244,000 pounds*
e. *none of the above*

39. Sarah bought a carton of 75 nails weighing $\frac{3}{4}$ of a pound. How much did each nail weigh?

a. *56 pounds*
b. *100 pounds*
c. *.01 pound*
d. *$\frac{1}{56}$ pound*
e. *$\frac{3}{100}$ pound*

40. Cynthia took 19 girls roller skating. If it cost $.75 for each of the children to get in and $.50 for each of them to rent skates, how much money did Cynthia have to collect?

a. *$20.25*
b. *$23.75*
c. *$17.75*
d. *$1.25*
e. *$4.75*

41. Oranges cost $1.50 a dozen. Winsome bought 4 oranges. How much money did she spend?

a. *$6.00*
b. *$1.54*
c. *$1.46*
d. *$.50*
e. *$4.50*

42. A $\frac{2}{3}$ majority of those voting in the House of Representatives is needed in order to override a presidential veto. If all 435 representatives vote, how many votes are needed to override a veto?

   a. *290 votes*
   b. *145 votes*
   c. *657 votes*
   d. *658 votes*
   e. *224 votes*

43. East Somerville has 948 homes. 12 people are collecting money for the Heart Association. If they all visit the same number of homes, how many homes should each of them visit?

   a. *960 homes*
   b. *936 homes*
   c. *79 homes*
   d. *11,376 homes*
   e. *none of the above*

44. Carol was told that she would have to pay $684 interest on a $3,600 loan. What interest rate would she have to pay?

   a. *$2,912*
   b. *$4,284*
   c. *19%*
   d. *5.3%*
   e. *81%*

45. Sears is offering 20% off on their $260 refrigerator. How much can you save by buying the refrigerator on sale?

   a. *$52*
   b. *$202*
   c. *$312*
   d. *$104*
   e. *none of the above*

46. A piece of cheese was labeled $1.79 a pound. The price of the cheese was $1.06. How much did the cheese weigh?

   a. *$2.85*
   b. *$.73*
   c. *1.69 pounds*
   d. *1.90 pounds*
   e. *.59 pound*

47. A $1\frac{1}{4}$ pound lobster costs $7.80. How much does it cost per pound?

    a. *$9.75*
    b. *$6.24*
    c. *$6.55*
    d. *$9.05*
    e. *$1.56*

48. A factory produces $\frac{7}{8}$-ton steel girders. How much steel does it need to produce 600 of these girders?

    a. *525 tons*
    b. *52.5 tons*
    c. *686 tons*
    d. *68.6 tons*
    e. *none of the above*

49. Steve's Ice Cream Store puts $\frac{1}{16}$ pound of whipped cream on every sundae. For how many sundaes will a 9-pound container of whipped cream last?

    a. *25 sundaes*
    b. *7 sundaes*
    c. *144 sundaes*
    d. *26 sundaes*
    e. *none of the above*

50. A linoleum tile is $\frac{3}{4}$-foot wide. In order to finish off the room, Ed needs a tile only $\frac{1}{3}$-foot wide. How much did he have to cut off the tile so that it would fit?

    a. $\frac{1}{2}$ *foot*
    b. $\frac{5}{12}$ *foot*
    c. $\frac{4}{7}$ *foot*
    d. $\frac{1}{4}$ *foot*
    e. $\frac{4}{9}$ *foot*

Answers on page 167.

ANSWER KEY

CHAPTER 1

Exercise 1

1. How much snow fell during the entire winter?
2. What is the total cooking time?
3. How much does it cost to park at the meter?
4. How many years did Joe serve in prison?

Exercise 2

1. numbers and labels: (124) commuters, (119) commuters
   label of the answer: commuters
2. numbers and labels: (7) waitresses, (56) tables
   label of the answer: tables
3. numbers and labels: (6) cents, $(1.47)
   label of the answer: $
4. numbers and labels: $(38), $(329)
   label of the answer: $
5. numbers and labels: (4) legs, (6) chairs
   label of the answer: legs

Exercise 3

1. *given information*: 22 years, 20 years, 23
   necessary information: (22 years) (20 years)
   You are only comparing Mona's age with her sister's age. Therefore, the boyfriend's age is not needed.
2. *given information*: $86, $67, 2 children
   necessary information: ($86) ($67)
   You do not need to know Rena's number of children in order to find the total amount of assistance she receives.
3. *given information*: three times, 20-year-old, 10 hours
   necessary information: (three times) (10 hours)
   You do not need to use Laura's age to find out how many hours Marilyn works.
4. *given information*: $43, 7-year-old, $39, 2 months
   necessary information: ($43) ($39)
   Although you would add the total for the 2 months, the number 2 is not needed in the solution nor is the age of the car.
5. *given information*: $2,460, $35,800, $1.20
   necessary information: ($2,460) ($1.20)
   The money made on shoes is not needed to determine how many gallons of oil were bought.
6. *given information*: 45, 8 people, half of the family
   necessary information: (8 people) (half of the family)
   Erma's age is not information needed to answer the question, "For how many people does Jack cook?"

7. *given information*: 4,700 workers, 3,900, 700 of the employees
   necessary information: (4,700) (700)
   In finding the number of employees currently working, the total number of skilled workers is not necessary information.

CHAPTER 2

Exercise 1

1. (plus)
2. (and) (altogether)
3. (sum) (and)
4. (added)
5. (increase)
6. (more) (altogether)

Exercise 2

1. (altogether)
   5 inches
   +23 inches
   28 inches
2. (increased)
   50 cents
   +20 cents
   70 cents
3. (total)
   3,500 pounds
   + 720 pounds
   4,220 pounds
4. (larger than)
   2 rooms
   +3 rooms
   5 room apartment
5. (and)
   $121,460
   +$ 89,742
   $211,202

Exercise 3

1. (cheaper than)
2. (decrease)
3. (less)
4. (difference)
5. (reduced)

Exercise 4

1. (left)
   105 homes
   − 36 homes
   69 homes
2. (change)
   $20
   − $16
   $ 4
3. (left)
   $361
   − $325
   $ 36
4. (difference)
   $12,635
   − $ 7,849
   $ 4,786
5. (fallen)
   86 degrees
   − 12 degrees
   74 degrees
   (The morning low of 58 degrees is not necessary information.)

ANSWER KEY (continued)

Exercise 5

1. (in all, and)
add

```
   5 cans
+  8 cans
  13 cans
```

2. (more than)
subtract

```
 26 pounds
-12 pounds
 14 pounds
```

3. (total, added)
add

```
 23 cans
+57 cans
 80 cans
```

4. (gaining)
add

```
  3,900 pounds
+   240 pounds
  4,140 pounds
```

5. (reduced)
subtract

```
  $345
- $ 68
  $277
```

6. (longer than)
subtract

```
 262 feet
- 38 feet
 224 feet
```

Exercise 6

1. (and, altogether)
add

```
  86 books
+ 53 books
 139 books
```

2. (more than)
subtract

```
 31 rings
-15 rings
 16 rings
```

3. (and, total)
add

```
 564 people
+365 people
 929 people
```

4. (decrease)
subtract

```
 421 units
-253 units
 168 units
```

5. (farther)
subtract

```
 10,000 miles
-  3,000 miles
  7,000 miles
```

(4 necklaces is not
necessary information.)

6. (increased)
add

```
 $230
+$ 35
 $265
```

CHAPTER 3

Exercise 1

1. (rose)
2. (rose)
3. (increase)
4. (decrease)
5. (less)

6. (less)
7. (lowered)
8. (raised)
9. (more)

Exercise 2

1. B
2. A
3. B

4. B
5. A

Exercise 3

1. *necessary information:* 320 pages, 205 pages
restatement: A.

```
  320 pages
+ 205 pages
  525 pages
```

2. *necessary information:* 24 bowls, 16 plates
restatement: A.

```
  24 bowls
+ 16 plates
  40 pieces
```

3. *necessary information:* 48,624 microwave ovens,
37,716 microwaves
restatement: B.

```
  48,624 microwave ovens
+ 37,716 microwaves
  86,340 microwaves
```

4. *necessary information:* 50,000 miles, 34,913
miles
restatement: B.

```
  50,000 miles
- 34,913 miles
  15,087 miles
```

Exercise 4

1.
```
  31 students
-  3 students
  28 students
```
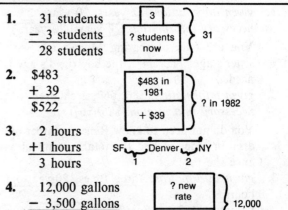

2.
```
  $483
+  39
  $522
```

3.
```
  2 hours
+ 1 hours
  3 hours
```

4.
```
  12,000 gallons
-  3,500 gallons
   8,500 gallons
```

(The age of the dam operator is not necessary
information.)

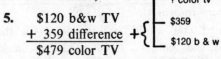

5.
```
  $120 b&w TV
+  359 difference
  $479 color TV
```

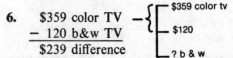

6.
```
  $359 color TV
-  120 b&w TV
  $239 difference
```

7.
```
  61° 11 p.m.
+ 13° decrease
  74° 6 p.m.
```

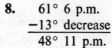

8.
```
  61° 6 p.m.
- 13° decrease
  48° 11 p.m.
```

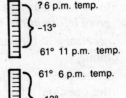

9. 1,412 graduates
  − 957 graduates living
     455 graduates have died

? died	
957 living	

} 1,412 people

10. $6,000
  −$3,800
   $2,200

? owed	
$3,800	

} $6,000

11. 46 cars
  +35 cars
   81 cars

35 cars	
46 cars	

} February sales

12. 2,600 pound truck
  +1,000 pound load
   3,600 pounds

1,000 lb.	
2,600 lb.	

} fully loaded truck

13. 29 students
  − 4 students
    25 students

? last year	4 students

⎵ 29 students

Exercise 5

1. *necessary information:* <u>13 cent stamp</u>, <u>quarter</u>
amount paid − price of stamp = amount of change
25 cents − 13 cents = amount of change
12 cents = amount of change

  25 cents
 −13 cents
  12 cents

2. *necessary information:* <u>32 miles</u>, <u>51 miles</u>
total miles driven − commuting distance = additional driving
51 miles − 32 miles = additional driving
19 miles = additional driving

  51 miles
 −32 miles
  19 miles

3. *necessary information:* <u>134 tickets</u>, <u>172 tickets</u>
ticket sales needed to break even − tickets sold = tickets to be sold
172 tickets − 134 tickets = tickets to be sold
38 tickets = tickets to be sold

  172 tickets
 −134 tickets
   38 tickets

4. *necessary information:* <u>$13</u>   <u>$460</u>
price of car − savings = loan
$1300 − $460 = loan
$840 = loan

  $1,300
 − $460
   $840

5. *necessary information:* <u>150 names</u>, <u>119 names</u>
names needed − names on first day = more names
150 names − 119 names = more names
31 names = more names

  150 names
 −119 names
   31 names

6. *necessary information:* <u>47 pounds</u>, <u>119</u>
new weight + weight loss = original weight
119 pounds + 47 pounds = original weight
166 pounds = original weight

  119 pounds
 + 47 pounds
  166 pounds

7. *necessary information:* <u>$13</u>, <u>$68</u>
new food stamp allotment + reduction = original amount
$68 + $13 = original amount
$81 = original amount

  $68
 +$13
  $81

8. *necessary information:* <u>$365</u>, <u>$279</u>
original price − sales price = savings
$365 − $279 = savings
$86 = savings

  $365
 −$279
  $86

9. *necessary information:* <u>$213</u>, <u>$185</u>
dollars withheld − amount owed = refund
$213 − $185 = refund
$28 = refund

  $213
 −$185
  $28

10. *necessary information:* <u>3,500 cars</u>, <u>8,200 cars</u>
new production + production cut = original production
8,200 cars + 3,500 cars = original production
11,700 cars = original production

  8,200 cars
 + 3,500 cars
  11,700 cars

11. *necessary information:* <u>$8,682</u>, <u>$7,991</u>
earnings − spending = savings
$8,682 − $7,991 = savings
$691 = savings

  $8,682
 −$7,991
  $691

ANSWER KEY (continued)
Exercise 5 continued

12. *necessary information:* <u>1,423 gallons</u>, <u>1,289 gallons</u>
Bertha + Calico = total gallons
1,423 gallons + 1,289 gallons = total gallons
2,712 gallons = total gallons

   1,423 gallons
<u>+1,289 gallons</u>
   2,712 gallons

13. *necessary information:* <u>72,070 seats</u>, <u>58,682 people</u>
seats − people = empty seats
72,070 seats − 58,682 people = empty seats
13,388 seats = empty seats

   72,070 seats
<u>−58,682 people</u>
   13,388 seats

14. *necessary information:* <u>49 days</u>, <u>56 days</u>
spinach days + green bean days = total days
49 days + 56 days = total days
105 days = total days

   49 days
<u>+ 56 days</u>
  105 days

CHAPTER 4

Exercise 1

1. C   **4.** D
2. B   **5.** F
3. A   **6.** E

Exercise 2

1. 10,000 people
2. 1,000,000 birds
3. 45,000 people
4. 22 pounds
5. 5 feet 5 inches

Exercise 3

1. F   **4.** D
2. E   **5.** A
3. C   **6.** B

Exercise 4

NOTE: Approximations may vary.
1. *restatement:* B
7.1 miles − 6.3 miles = .8 mile
approximation: 7 miles − 6 miles = 1 mile

2. *restatement:* A
9.4 gallons + 14.7 gallons = 24.1 gallons
approximation: 9 gallons + 15 gallons = 24 gallons

(The fact that the car is 8 years old is not necessary information.)

3. *restatement:* A
1.42 pounds + .98 pound = 2.40 pounds
approximation: 1.5 pounds + 1 pound = 2.5 pounds

4. *restatement:* B
200.15 mph − 198.7 mph = 1.45 mph
approximation: 200 mph − 199 mph = 1 mph

5. *restatement:* B
9.1% − 7.9% = 1.2%
approximation: 9% − 8% = 1%

6. *restatement:* A
12.6 pounds − 3.82 pounds = 8.78 pounds
approximation: 13 pounds − 4 pounds = 9 pounds

7. *restatement:* B
.7 inch + .375 inch = 1.075 inches
approximation: .7 inch + .4 inch = 1.1 inches

Exercise 5

1. $1.60
  <u>+ .25</u>
  $1.85

2.   .70 gram
  <u>−.55 gram</u>
  .15 gram

3.   .342
  <u>−.083</u>
  .259

4. $113.50
  <u>− 26.13</u>
  $ 87.37

5.   1.60 inches
  <u>− .05 inch</u>
  1.55 inches

(The length of 3.2 inches is not necessary information.)

6. $46.65
  <u>+23.35</u>
  $70.00

7.   .080 inch
  <u>+.015 inch</u>
  .095 inch allowable gap

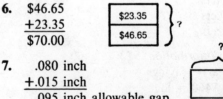

8.   126.40 tons
  <u>− 18.64 tons</u>
  107.76 tons

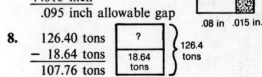

Exercise 6

1. *necessary information:* .6 ounce, 2.4 ounces
new weight + reduction = original weight
2.4 ounces + .6 ounce = original weight
3.0 ounces = original weight

$$\begin{array}{r} 2.4 \text{ ounces} \\ +\ .6 \text{ ounce} \\ \hline 3.0 \text{ ounces} \end{array}$$

2. *necessary information:* $2.38, $10.00
amount paid − lunch cost = change
$10.00 − $2.38 = change
$7.62 = change

$$\begin{array}{r} \$10.00 \\ -\$\ 2.38 \\ \hline \$\ 7.62 \end{array}$$

3. *necessary information:* 3.94 pounds, 4.68 pounds
first chicken + second chicken = total weight
3.94 pounds + 4.68 pounds = total weight
8.62 pounds = total weight

$$\begin{array}{r} 3.94 \text{ pounds} \\ +4.68 \text{ pounds} \\ \hline 8.62 \text{ pounds} \end{array}$$

(The 1.32 pound steak is not necessary information.)

4. *necessary information:* 23,172.3 miles, 23,391.4 miles
reading at end − reading at start = length of trip
23,391.4 miles − 23,172.3 miles = length of trip
219.1 miles = length of trip

$$\begin{array}{r} 23,391.4 \text{ miles} \\ -23,172.3 \text{ miles} \\ \hline 219.1 \text{ miles} \end{array}$$

5. *necessary information:* $.40, $.65
bus + subway = one-way trip
$.40 + $.65 = one-way trip
$1.05 = one-way trip

$$\begin{array}{r} \$\ .40 \\ +\$\ .65 \\ \hline \$1.05 \end{array}$$

6. *necessary information* $341.98, $335.26
Massachusetts − New Hampshire = savings
$341.98 − $335.26 = savings
$6.72 = savings

$$\begin{array}{r} \$341.98 \\ -\$335.26 \\ \hline \$6.7 \end{array}$$

7. *necessary information:* 14.36 seconds, 13.9 seconds
first 100 meters + second 100 meters = total time
14.36 seconds + 13.9 seconds = total time
28.26 seconds = total time

$$\begin{array}{r} 14.36 \text{ seconds} \\ +13.9\ \ \text{ seconds} \\ \hline 28.26 \text{ seconds} \end{array}$$

(The lengths for the race—100 meters and 200 meters—are not necessary information. They are not used in the arithmetic.)

Exercise 7

1. B
$$\begin{array}{r} 28\frac{1}{2} = \quad 28\frac{2}{4} \text{ inches} \\ +31\frac{1}{4} = +31\frac{1}{4} \text{ inches} \\ \hline 59\frac{3}{4} \text{ inches} \end{array}$$

2. A
$$\begin{array}{r} 1\frac{2}{3} \text{ cups} \\ +1\frac{1}{3} \text{ cups} \\ \hline 2\frac{3}{3} = 3 \text{ cups} \end{array}$$

(2-quart mixing bowl is unnecessary information.)

3. A
$$\begin{array}{r} 71\frac{1}{4} = \quad 71\frac{1}{4} = \quad 70\frac{5}{4} \text{ pounds} \\ -62\frac{1}{2} = -62\frac{2}{4} = -62\frac{2}{4} \text{ pounds} \\ \hline 8\frac{3}{4} \text{ pounds} \end{array}$$

4. B
$$\begin{array}{r} 23\frac{1}{4} = \quad 22\frac{5}{4} \text{ inches} \\ -18\frac{3}{4} = -18\frac{3}{4} \text{ inches} \\ \hline 4\frac{2}{4} \text{ inches} = 4\frac{1}{2} \text{ inches} \end{array}$$

Exercise 8

1.
$$\begin{array}{r} 4 = \quad 3\frac{8}{8} \text{ inches} \\ -\frac{5}{8} = -\ \frac{5}{8} \text{ inches} \\ \hline 3\frac{3}{8} \text{ inches} \end{array}$$

(The measurement, 2 inches, is not needed to solve the problem.)

2.
$$\begin{array}{r} 8\frac{1}{2} = \quad 8\frac{2}{4} = \quad 7\frac{6}{4} \text{ hours} \\ -1\frac{3}{4} = -1\frac{3}{4} = -1\frac{3}{4} \text{ hours} \\ \hline 6\frac{3}{4} \text{ hours} \end{array}$$

ANSWER KEY (continued)

Exercise 8 continued

3. $\quad 6\frac{1}{2} = 6\frac{2}{4}$ hours

$\quad +\frac{3}{4} = +\frac{3}{4}$ hour

$\quad\quad\quad 6\frac{5}{4} = 7\frac{1}{4}$ hours

4. $\quad\quad 2 = 1\frac{2}{2}$ inches

$\quad -\frac{1}{2} = -\frac{1}{2}$ inch

$\quad\quad\quad 1\frac{1}{2}$ inches

(The measurement, 4 inches, is not needed to solve the problem.)

5. $\quad 2\frac{1}{2} = 2\frac{3}{6} = 1\frac{9}{6}$ cups

$\quad -1\frac{2}{3} = -1\frac{4}{6} = -1\frac{4}{6}$ cups

$\quad\quad\quad\quad\quad\quad\quad \frac{5}{6}$ cup

Exercise 9

1. bowl − rum = other ingredients

3 quarts − $1\frac{1}{4}$ quarts = other ingredients

$1\frac{3}{4}$ quarts = other ingredients

$\quad\quad 3 = \quad 2\frac{4}{4}$ quarts

$\quad -1\frac{1}{4} = -1\frac{1}{4}$ quarts

$\quad\quad\quad\quad 1\frac{3}{4}$ quarts

2. original length − new length = amount taken off

$34\frac{1}{2}$ inches − $32\frac{3}{4}$ inches = amount taken off

$1\frac{3}{4}$ inches = amount taken off

$\quad 34\frac{1}{2} = \quad 33\frac{6}{4}$ inches

$\quad -32\frac{3}{4} = -32\frac{3}{4}$ inches

$\quad\quad\quad\quad 1\frac{3}{4}$ inches

3. original amount − amount sold = amount left

$6\frac{1}{2}$ yards − $3\frac{2}{3}$ yards = amount left

$2\frac{5}{6}$ yards = amount left

$\quad 6\frac{1}{2} = \quad 5\frac{9}{6}$ yards

$\quad -3\frac{2}{3} = -3\frac{4}{6}$ yards

$\quad\quad\quad\quad 2\frac{5}{6}$ yards

(3 weeks in the store and 20 yards long are not necessary information.)

4. beef + pork = meat

$1\frac{1}{2}$ pounds + $\frac{3}{4}$ pound = meat

$2\frac{1}{4}$ pounds = meat

$\quad 1\frac{1}{2} = 1\frac{2}{4}$ pounds

$\quad +\frac{3}{4} = \frac{3}{4}$ pound

$\quad\quad 1\frac{5}{4} = 2\frac{1}{4}$ pounds

5. first week + second week = total wood

$\frac{1}{8}$ cord + $\frac{1}{12}$ cord = total wood

$\frac{5}{24}$ cord = total wood

$\quad \frac{1}{8} = \frac{3}{24}$ cord

$\quad +\frac{1}{12} = \frac{2}{24}$ cord

$\quad\quad\quad = \frac{5}{24}$ cord

6. total cloth − hem = drape

$62\frac{1}{2} − \frac{3}{4}$ = drape

$61\frac{3}{4}$ inches = drape

$\quad 62\frac{1}{2} = 61\frac{6}{4}$ inches

$\quad -\frac{3}{4} = -\frac{3}{4}$ inches

$\quad\quad\quad 61\frac{3}{4}$ inches

Exercise 10

1. b.

subtract: 55,572 nails

$\quad\quad$ − 1,263 nails

$\quad\quad\quad$ 54,309 nails

(The number of screws is not necessary information.)

2. b.

subtract: $75.62

$\quad\quad$ − $38.56

$\quad\quad\quad$ $37.06

3. d.

subtract: 19.1 miles per gallon

$\quad\quad$ −16.2 miles per gallon

$\quad\quad\quad$ 2.9 miles per gallon

4. d.

add: $\quad$ $ 800

$\quad\quad$ + $2,400

$\quad\quad\quad$ $3,200

(The amount left in her savings account is not necessary information.)

5. c.

subtract: $\frac{1}{4}$ pound = $\frac{4}{16}$ pound

$\quad\quad -\frac{3}{16}$ pound = $-\frac{3}{16}$ pound

$\quad\quad\quad\quad\quad\quad\quad \frac{1}{16}$ pound

6. c.

subtract: .6 gram

$\quad\quad$ − .47 gram

$\quad\quad\quad$ .13 gram

(The number .5 is not necessary information.)

7. a.

add: $391,445

$\quad$ + $528,555

$\quad\quad$ $920,000

8. b.

add: $26\frac{3}{4}$ inches = $26\frac{6}{8}$ inches

+ $2\frac{3}{8}$ inches = $2\frac{3}{8}$ inches

$28\frac{9}{8}$ inches = $29\frac{1}{8}$ inches

9. e.

add: $\frac{5}{8}$ cord = $\frac{15}{24}$ cord

+ $\frac{1}{12}$ cord = $\frac{2}{24}$ cord

$\frac{17}{24}$ cord

10. e.

subtract: 5.15 tubes

− 3.4 tubes

1.75 tubes

11. c.

subtract: 420,000 acres

−   96,500 acres

323,500 acres

(The question does not call for using the third leasing.)

12. d.

add: 420,000 acres

96,500 acres

+ 123,460 acres

639,960 acres

13. b.

add: $\frac{1}{2}$ radioactivity = $\frac{8}{16}$ radioactivity

+ $\frac{7}{16}$ radioactivity = $\frac{7}{16}$ radioactivity

$\frac{15}{16}$ radioactivity

14. c.

add: $\frac{3}{4}$ ounce = $\frac{9}{12}$ ounce

+ $\frac{1}{3}$ ounce = $\frac{4}{12}$ ounce

$\frac{13}{12}$ = $1\frac{1}{12}$ ounce

15. d.

add: 2.77 grams

+ .03 gram

2.8 grams

CHAPTER 5

Exercise 1

1. (times)
2. (per)
3. (total) (also an addition key word)
4. (twice)

Exercise 2

1. *necessary information:* 42 cents, twice
    key words: (twice as much)

42 cents

× 2

84 cents

2. *necessary information:* 4 sets, 6 strings
    key word: (per)

4 sets

× 6 strings

24 strings

3. *necessary information:* 5 times a day, week
    key word: (times)

5 times a day

× 7 days (week)

35 times

(Twelve newspapers is not necessary information.)

4. *necessary information:* 8 ounces, 473 regular-size sodas
    key word: (total)

473 regular size sodas

×   8 ounces

3,784 ounces

5. *necessary information:* $47, 3 hours
    key word: (per)

$ 47

×   3 hours

$141

Exercise 3

1. (split) (evenly) (each)
2. (each) (each)
3. (average) (each)
4. (shared) (evenly) (each)

Exercise 4

1. *necessary information:* 12 oz., 4 children
    key words: (shared evenly) (each)
    12 oz. ÷ 4 children

$$\frac{3}{4)12}$$

3 oz. per child

2. *necessary information:* 60-minute hockey game, 3 equal periods
    key words: (divided) (equal) (periods), (each)
    60-minute hockey game ÷ 3 equal periods

$$\frac{20}{3)60}$$

20 minutes

ANSWER KEY (continued)

Exercise 4 continued

3. *necessary information:* <u>$156</u>, <u>12 monthly payments</u>
key word: (each)
$156 ÷ 12 monthly payments

$$12\overline{)156}\overset{13}{}$$

$13

(The $319 cost for a new washing machine is not necessary information.)

4. *necessary information:* <u>24 cigarettes</u>, <u>96 cents</u>
key word: (each)
96 cents ÷ 24 cigarettes

$$24\overline{)96}\overset{4}{}$$

4 cents

5. *necessary information:* <u>$3</u>, <u>$4,629</u>
key words: (each), (even)
$4,629 ÷ $3

$$3\overline{)4,629}\overset{1,543}{}$$

1,543 tickets

6. *necessary information:* <u>14 taxis</u>, <u>336 gallons</u>
key words: (average), (each)
336 gallons ÷ 14 taxis

$$14\overline{)336}\overset{24}{}$$

24 gallons

Exercise 5

1. *division key words:* (divided), (evenly), (each)

$$4\overline{)8}\overset{2}{}$$

2 slices

2. *division key words:* (each), (split evenly)

$$5\overline{)90,000}\overset{18,000}{}$$

$18,000

3. *multiplication key words:* (per), (total)

$$\begin{array}{r} 12 \\ \times 15 \\ \hline 180 \end{array}$$

$180

4. *multiplication key word:* (twice)

$$\begin{array}{r} 2\ \\ \times 2 \\ \hline 54 \end{array}$$

$54

5. *division key words:* (each), (average)

$$5\overline{)225}\overset{45}{}$$

45 points
(35 points is unnecessary information.)

---

6. *division key words:* (average) (each)

$$12\overline{)48}\overset{4}{}$$

4 inches per month

7. *division key words:* (cut) (equal pieces) (each)

$$175\overline{)3,500}\overset{20}{}$$

20 grams

Exercise 6

1. part: 78 cartons
part: 50 cups

$$\begin{array}{r} 78 \\ \times 50 \\ \hline 3,900 \end{array}$$

total: 3,900 cups

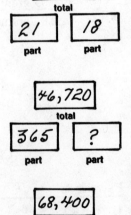

2. part: 30 days
part: $6 a day

$$\begin{array}{r} 30 \\ \times 6 \\ \hline 180 \end{array}$$

total: $180

3. part: 780,000 copies
part: 140 pages

$$\begin{array}{r} 780,000 \\ \times 140 \\ \hline 109,200,000 \end{array}$$

total: 109,200,000 pages
(The length of the evening edition, 132 pages, is not necessary information.)

4. part: 2,400 square feet
total: 168,000 square feet

$$2,400\overline{)168,000}\overset{70}{}$$

part: 70 pints

5. part: 21 gallons
part: 18 miles per gallon

$$\begin{array}{r} 21 \\ \times 18 \\ \hline 378 \end{array}$$

total: 378 miles

6. part: 365 days in a year
total: 46,720 people

$$*365\overline{)46,720}\overset{128}{}$$

part: 128 people a day
*365 days in a year

7. part: 150 nails
total: 68,400 nails

$$150\overline{)68,400}\overset{456}{}$$

part: 456 boxes

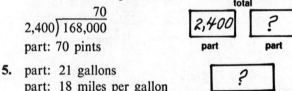

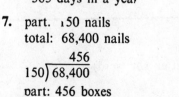

8. part: 12 hours
   total: 3,852 hamburgers

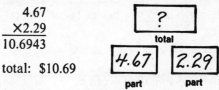

$$\begin{array}{r} 321 \\ 12\overline{)3852} \end{array}$$

   part: 321 hamburgers per hour

9. part: 27,429 packets
   part: 35 seeds per packet

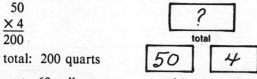

$$\begin{array}{r} 27,429 \\ \times\ 35 \\ \hline 960,015 \end{array}$$

   total: 960,015 seeds

10. part: 12 packs
    total: 32,784 packs

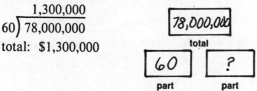

$$\begin{array}{r} 2,732 \\ 12\overline{)32,784} \end{array}$$

    part: 2,732 cartons
    (8 ounces is unnecessary information.)

11. part: 4 quarts in a gallon
    part: 50 gallon
    number of gallons × quarts in a gallon =
    total number of quarts

$$\begin{array}{r} 50 \\ \times\ 4 \\ \hline 200 \end{array}$$

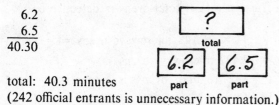

    total: 200 quarts

12. part: 60 colleges
    total: $78,000,000
    total amount of money ÷ number of colleges
    = amount of money for each college

$$\begin{array}{r} 1,300,000 \\ 60\overline{)78,000,000} \end{array}$$

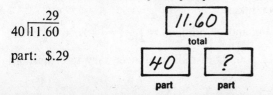

    total: $1,300,000

CHAPTER 6

Exercise 1

1. miles × minutes per mile = total minutes
   6.2 miles × 6.5 minutes per mile = total minutes

$$\begin{array}{r} 6.2 \\ 6.5 \\ \hline 40.30 \end{array}$$

   total: 40.3 minutes
   (242 official entrants is unnecessary information.)

2. total price ÷ number of pounds = price per pound
   $11.60 ÷ 40 pounds = price per pound

$$\begin{array}{r} .29 \\ 40\overline{)11.60} \end{array}$$

   part: $.29

3. total miles ÷ gallons = miles per gallon
   159.75 miles ÷ 7.1 gallons = miles per gallon

$$\begin{array}{r} 22.5 \\ 7.1.\overline{)159.7.5} \end{array}$$

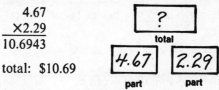

   part: 22.5 miles per gallon

4. number of pounds × price per pound = total price
   4.67 pounds × $2.29 per pound = total price

$$\begin{array}{r} 4.67 \\ \times 2.29 \\ \hline 10.6943 \end{array}$$

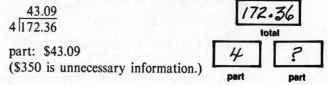

   total: $10.69

5. food bill ÷ roommates = price per roommate
   $172.36 ÷ 4 roommates = price per roommate

$$\begin{array}{r} 43.09 \\ 4\overline{)172.36} \end{array}$$

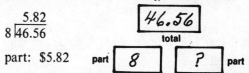

   part: $43.09
   ($350 is unnecessary information.)

6. total commission ÷ hours = average commission
   $46.56 ÷ 8 hours = average commission

$$\begin{array}{r} 5.82 \\ 8\overline{)46.56} \end{array}$$

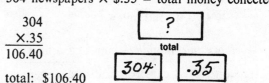

   part: $5.82

7. newspapers × price of each newspaper = total
   money
   304 newspapers × $.35 = total money collected

$$\begin{array}{r} 304 \\ \times .35 \\ \hline 106.40 \end{array}$$

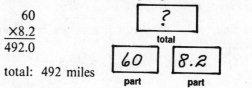

   total: $106.40

8. gallons × miles per gallon = total miles
   60 gallons × 8.2 miles per gallon = total miles

$$\begin{array}{r} 60 \\ \times 8.2 \\ \hline 492.0 \end{array}$$

   total: 492 miles

Exercise 2

1. *necessary information:* $\frac{2}{3}$ of, 36 inches

   fraction (of) × total precipitation = inches of rain
   $\frac{2}{3}$ × 36 inches $= \frac{2}{\cancel{3}_1} \times \frac{\cancel{36}^{12}}{1} = 24$ inches

2. *necessary information:* $\frac{7}{8}$ of, 23,352 accidents

   fraction (of) × total accidents = accidents in urban areas
   $\frac{7}{8}$ (of) × 23,352 accidents =
   $\frac{7}{\cancel{8}_1} \times \frac{\cancel{23,352}^{2,919}}{1} = 20,433$ accidents

ANSWER KEY (continued)

Exercise 2 continued

3. *necessary information:* $7\frac{2}{3}$ pounds, 10 boxes

   pounds per box × number of boxes = total pounds

   $7\frac{2}{3} \times 10 = \frac{23}{3} \times \frac{10}{1} = \frac{230}{3} = 76\frac{2}{3}$ pounds

4. *necessary information:* $\frac{2}{3}$ can of, 12 days

   cans per day × number of days = total cans

   $\frac{2}{3}$ can × 12 days = $\frac{2}{3} \times \frac{\cancel{12}^{4}}{1} = 8$ cans

   (2 dog biscuits is unnecessary information.)

5. *necessary information:* $1\frac{1}{8}$ ounces, $3\frac{1}{2}$ candy bars

   ounces per candy bar × number of candy bars = total ounces

   $1\frac{1}{8}$ ounces × $3\frac{1}{2}$ candy bars =

   $\frac{9}{8} \times \frac{7}{2} = \frac{63}{16} = 3\frac{15}{16}$ ounces

6. *necessary information:* 17,000 miles per hour, 2½ hours

   miles per hour × number of hours = total miles

   17,000 miles per hour × $2\frac{1}{2}$ hours=

   $\frac{\cancel{17{,}000}^{8{,}500}}{1} \times \frac{5}{\cancel{2}_{1}} = 42{,}500$ miles

7. *necessary information:* $\frac{1}{2}$ cup, $\frac{1}{2}$ of a load

   fraction (of) × cups per load = detergent needed

   $\frac{1}{2}$ (of) × $\frac{1}{2}$ cup = $\frac{1}{2} \times \frac{1}{2} = \frac{1}{4}$ cup

8. *necessary information:* $\frac{2}{5}$ of, $\frac{1}{4}$ pound

   fraction (of) × weight of hamburger = amount of fat

   $\frac{2}{5}$ (of) × $\frac{1}{4}$ pound = $\frac{\cancel{2}^{1}}{5} \times \frac{1}{\cancel{4}_{2}} = \frac{1}{10}$ pound

Exercise 3

1. *necessary information:* $22\frac{1}{2}$ inches, $\frac{5}{8}$ inch

   depth of box ÷ thickness of each book = number of books

   $22\frac{1}{2}$ inches ÷ $\frac{5}{8}$ inch = $\frac{\cancel{45}^{9}}{\cancel{2}_{1}} \times \frac{\cancel{8}^{4}}{\cancel{5}_{1}} = 36$ books

2. *necessary information:* 13 people, $6\frac{1}{2}$ pounds

   total amount of meat ÷ number of people = size of a portion

   $6\frac{1}{2}$ pounds ÷ 13 people = $\frac{\cancel{13}^{1}}{2} \times \frac{1}{\cancel{13}_{1}} = \frac{1}{2}$ pound

3. *necessary information:* $2\frac{1}{4}$ feet, $265\frac{1}{2}$ feet

   total ribbon ÷ ribbon per book = number of books

   $265\frac{1}{2}$ feet ÷ $2\frac{1}{4}$ feet = $\frac{531}{2} \div \frac{9}{4} =$

   $\frac{\cancel{531}^{59}}{\cancel{2}_{1}} \times \frac{\cancel{4}^{2}}{\cancel{9}_{1}} = \frac{59}{1} \times \frac{2}{1} = 118$ books

4. *necessary information:* $8\frac{1}{2}$ pounds, $\frac{1}{4}$ pound

   total mashed potatoes ÷ potatoes per serving = number of servings

   $8\frac{1}{2}$ pounds ÷ $\frac{1}{4}$ pound = $\frac{17}{\cancel{2}_{1}} \times \frac{\cancel{4}^{2}}{1} = 34$ servings

   ($\frac{1}{3}$-pound green bean servings is not necessary information.)

5. *necessary information:* $9\frac{3}{4}$ ounces, 3 equal servings

   total peaches ÷ number of servings = size of each serving

   $9\frac{3}{4}$ ounces ÷ 3 servings = $\frac{\cancel{39}^{13}}{4} \times \frac{1}{\cancel{3}_{1}} =$

   $\frac{13}{4} = 3\frac{1}{4}$ ounces

Exercise 4

1. *necessary information:* 12 hours, $\frac{3}{4}$ hour

   total hours ÷ length of a session = number of sessions

   12 hours ÷ $\frac{3}{4}$ hour = $\frac{\cancel{12}^{4}}{1} \times \frac{4}{\cancel{3}_{1}} = 16$ sessions

2. *necessary information:* $\frac{2}{3}$ hour, 30 cars

   time per car × number of cars = total hours

   $\frac{2}{3}$ hour × 30 cars = $\frac{2}{\cancel{3}_{1}} \times \frac{\cancel{30}^{10}}{1} = 20$ hours

3. *necessary information:* $\frac{2}{3}$ hour, 24 hours

   total hours ÷ time per car = number of cars

   24 hours ÷ $\frac{2}{3}$ hour = $\frac{\cancel{24}^{12}}{1} \times \frac{3}{\cancel{2}_{1}} = 36$ cars

4. *necessary information:* $\frac{2}{3}$ of, 26,148 microwave ovens

   fraction (of) × total ovens = defective ovens

   $\frac{2}{3}$ (of) × 26,148 microwave ovens = $\frac{2}{\cancel{3}_{1}} \times \frac{\cancel{26{,}148}^{8{,}716}}{1}$

   = 17,432 microwave ovens

   (59,882 regular ovens is unnecessary information.)

5. *necessary information:* 6 hikers, $4\frac{1}{2}$ pounds

   total chocolate ÷ number of hikers = chocolate per hiker

   $4\frac{1}{2}$ pounds ÷ 6 hikers = $\frac{9}{2} \div \frac{6}{1} = \frac{\cancel{9}^{3}}{2} \times \frac{1}{\cancel{6}_{2}} = \frac{3}{4}$ pound

   ($1\frac{3}{4}$ pounds of milk is unnecessary information.)

Exercise 5

1. b.

total weight ÷ weight of each jar = number of jars

40 pounds ÷ $\frac{5}{8}$ pound = $\frac{\overset{8}{40}}{1} \times \frac{8}{\underset{1}{5}}$ = 64 jars

(The weight of a jar, $\frac{1}{8}$ pound, is not necessary information.)

2. c.

total cost ÷ square feet = cost per square foot

$20.80 ÷ 32 square feet = $.65

$$32\overline{)20.80}^{\,.65}$$

3. b.

fraction (of) × total raffle tickets = raffle sales needed

$\frac{1}{6}$ (of) × 3,000 raffle tickets =

$\frac{1}{\underset{1}{6}} \times \frac{\overset{500}{3,000}}{1}$ = 500 raffle tickets

4. b.

fraction (of) × winner's share = trainer's share

$\frac{3}{5}$ (of) × $17,490 = $\frac{3}{\underset{1}{5}} \times \frac{\overset{3,498}{17,490}}{1}$ = $10,494

(40 shares is unnecessary information.)

5. d.

total material ÷ material per apron = number of aprons

$7\frac{1}{3}$ yards ÷ $\frac{2}{3}$ yard/apron =

$\frac{22}{3} \div \frac{2}{3} = \frac{\overset{11}{22}}{\underset{1}{3}} \times \frac{\overset{1}{3}}{\underset{1}{2}}$ = 11 aprons

6. d.

total distance ÷ hours = miles per hour

263.1 miles ÷ 4.5 hours = 58.5 miles per hour

$$4.5\overline{)263.1}^{\,58.46} = 58.5$$

(8.1 gallons is unnecessary information.)

7. c.

total records ÷ records per box = number of boxes

1,410 records ÷ 30 records = 47 boxes

$$30\overline{)1410}^{\,47}$$

8. b.

number of kilometers × miles per kilometer = number of miles

15 kilometers × 62 miles per kilometer = 9.3 miles

$$\begin{array}{r} 15 \\ \underline{.62} \\ 9.30 \end{array}$$

CHAPTER 7

Exercise 1

2. $\dfrac{\text{2 teachers}}{\text{30 students}}$

3. $\dfrac{\text{40 dollars}}{\text{8 hours}}$

4. $\dfrac{\text{38 miles}}{\text{2 gallons}}$

5. $\dfrac{\text{3 buses}}{\text{114 commuters}}$

Exercise 2

1. $\dfrac{160 \text{ miles}}{5 \text{ hours}} = \dfrac{n}{10 \text{ hours}}$

$5 \times n = 160 \times 10$

$5n = 1600$

$n = \dfrac{1600}{5}$

$n = 320$ miles

2. $\dfrac{12 \text{ cars}}{32 \text{ people}} = \dfrac{3 \text{ cars}}{n}$

$12 \times n = 32 \times 3$

$12n = 96$

$n = \dfrac{96}{12}$

$n = 8$ people

3. $\dfrac{n}{8 \text{ quarters}} = \dfrac{6 \text{ dollars}}{24 \text{ quarters}}$

$24 \times n = 8 \times 6$

$24n = 48$

$n = \dfrac{48}{24}$

$n = 2$ dollars

4. $\dfrac{42 \text{ pounds}}{n} = \dfrac{14 \text{ pounds}}{4 \text{ chickens}}$

$14 \times n = 42 \times 4$

$14n = 168$

$n = \dfrac{168}{14}$

$n = 12$ chickens

5. $\dfrac{28,928 \text{ people}}{8 \text{ doctors}} = \dfrac{n}{1 \text{ doctor}}$

$8 \times n = 1 \times 28,928$

$8n = 28,928$

$n = \dfrac{28,928}{8}$

$n = 3,616$ people

ANSWER KEY (continued)

Exercise 2 continued

6. $\dfrac{\$4.39}{1 \text{ shirt}} = \dfrac{n}{6 \text{ shirts}}$

$1 \times n = \$4.39 \times 6$

$n = \$26.34$

7. $\dfrac{\$17.85}{3 \text{ shirts}} = \dfrac{n}{10 \text{ shirts}}$

$3 \times n = 17.85 \times 10$

$3n = 178.50$

$n = \dfrac{178.50}{3}$

$n = \$59.50$

8. $\dfrac{3 \text{ minutes}}{\frac{1}{2} \text{ mile}} = \dfrac{n}{5 \text{ miles}}$

$\frac{1}{2} \times n = 3 \times 5$

$\frac{1}{2}n = 15$

$n = 15 \div \frac{1}{2} = 15 \times 2$

$n = 30 \text{ minutes}$

9. $\dfrac{575 \text{ passengers}}{n \text{ days}} = \dfrac{1,725 \text{ passengers}}{21 \text{ days}}$

$1,725 \times n = 575 \times 21$

$1,725n = 12,075$

$n = \dfrac{12,075}{1,725}$

$n = 7 \text{ days}$

10. $\dfrac{7 \text{ blinks}}{\frac{1}{10} \text{ minute}} = \dfrac{n \text{ blinks}}{10 \text{ minutes}}$

$\frac{1}{10} \times n = 7 \times 10$

$\frac{1}{10} n = 70$

$n = 70 \times 10$

$n = 700 \text{ blinks}$

Exercise 3

1. *necessary information*: <u>7,800 people</u>, <u>140,400 people</u>

labels for proportion: $\dfrac{\text{shipments}}{\text{people}}$

$\dfrac{1 \text{ shipment}}{7,800 \text{ people}} = \dfrac{n \text{ shipments}}{140,400 \text{ people}}$

$7,800 \times n = 1 \times 140,400$

$n = \dfrac{140,400}{7,800}$

$n = 18 \text{ shipments}$

2. *necessary information*: <u>$340</u>, <u>24 hours</u>

labels for proportion: $\dfrac{\$}{\text{hour}}$

$\dfrac{\$340}{1 \text{ hour}} = \dfrac{\$ n}{24 \text{ hours}}$

$1 \times n = 340 \times 24$

$n = \$8,160$

(1,000-watt is unnecessary information.)

3. *necessary information*: <u>11 ounces</u>, <u>28 cans</u>

labels for proportion: $\dfrac{\text{ounces}}{\text{can}}$

$\dfrac{11 \text{ ounces}}{1 \text{ can}} = \dfrac{n \text{ ounces}}{28 \text{ cans}}$

$1 \times n = 11 \times 28$

$n = 308 \text{ ounces}$

4. *necessary information*: <u>52 words per minute</u>, <u>26 minutes</u>

labels for proportion: $\dfrac{\text{words}}{\text{minutes}}$

$\dfrac{52 \text{ words}}{1 \text{ minute}} = \dfrac{n \text{ words}}{26 \text{ minutes}}$

$1 \times n = 52 \times 26$

$n = 1,352 \text{ words}$

5. *necessary information*: <u>3,960 Band-Aids</u>, <u>180 school days</u>

labels for proportion: $\dfrac{\text{Band-Aids}}{\text{school days}}$

$\dfrac{3,960 \text{ Band-Aids}}{180 \text{ school days}} = \dfrac{n \text{ Band-Aids}}{1 \text{ school day}}$

$180 \times n = 1 \times 3,960$

$180n = 3,960$

$n = \dfrac{3,960}{180}$

$n = 22 \text{ Band-Aids}$

6. *necessary information*: <u>5,460 aspirins</u>, <u>260 aspirins</u>

labels for proportion: $\dfrac{\text{aspirins}}{\text{bottles}}$

$\dfrac{260 \text{ aspirins}}{1 \text{ bottle}} = \dfrac{5,460 \text{ aspirins}}{n \text{ bottles}}$

$260 \times n = 1 \times 5,460$

$260n = 5,460$

$n = \dfrac{5,460}{260}$

$n = 21$

(720 antacid tablets is unnecessary information.)

7. *necessary information*: <u>126 tons</u>, <u>3 tons</u>
    labels for proportion: $\dfrac{\text{tons}}{\text{trip}}$

    $\dfrac{3 \text{ tons}}{1 \text{ trip}} = \dfrac{126 \text{ tons}}{n \text{ trips}}$
    $3 \times n = 1 \times 126$
    $3n = 126$
    $n = \dfrac{126}{3}$
    $n = 42$ trips

8. *necessary information*: <u>18 feet</u>, <u>3 feet in a yard</u>

    labels for proportion: $\dfrac{\text{feet}}{\text{yards}}$

    $\dfrac{3 \text{ feet}}{1 \text{ yard}} = \dfrac{18 \text{ feet}}{n \text{ yards}}$
    $3 \times n = 18 \times 1$
    $3n = 18$
    $n = \dfrac{18}{3}$
    $n = 6$ yards

9. *necessary information*: <u>26 waterchestnuts</u>, <u>three cans</u>

    labels for proportion: $\dfrac{\text{waterchestnuts}}{\text{cans}}$
    $\dfrac{26 \text{ waterchestnuts}}{1 \text{ can}} = \dfrac{n \text{ waterchestnuts}}{3 \text{ cans}}$

    $1 \times n = 3 \times 26$
    $n = 78$ waterchestnuts
    (Six ounces in a can is unnecessary information.)

Exercise 4

1. *necessary information*: <u>25.4 millimeters</u>, <u>100 millimeter</u>
    labels for proportion: $\dfrac{\text{millimeters}}{\text{inch}}$

    $\dfrac{25.4 \text{ millimeters}}{1 \text{ inch}} = \dfrac{100 \text{ millimeters}}{n \text{ inches}}$
    $25.4 \times n = 1 \times 100$
    $25.4n = 100$
    $n = \dfrac{100}{25.4}$
    $n = 3.94$ inches

2. *necessary information*: <u>2.2 pounds</u>, <u>36 kilograms</u>
    labels for proportion: $\dfrac{\text{pounds}}{\text{kilograms}}$
    $\dfrac{2.2 \text{ pounds}}{1 \text{ kilogram}} = \dfrac{n \text{ pounds}}{36 \text{ kilograms}}$
    $1 \times n = 2.2 \times 36$
    $n = 79.2$ pounds

3. *necessary information*: <u>35.5 hours</u>, <u>$4.62</u>
    labels for proportion: $\dfrac{\text{hours}}{\$}$
    $\dfrac{35.5 \text{ hours}}{\$n} = \dfrac{1 \text{ hour}}{\$4.62}$
    $1 \times n = 35.5 \times 4.62$
    $n = \$164.01$

4. *necessary information*: <u>1.09 yards</u>, <u>880 yards</u>
    labels for proportion: $\dfrac{\text{yards}}{\text{meter}}$
    $\dfrac{1.09 \text{ yards}}{1 \text{ meter}} = \dfrac{880 \text{ yards}}{n \text{ meters}}$
    $1.09 \times n = 1 \times 880$
    $1.09n = 880$
    $n = \dfrac{880}{1.09}$
    $n = 807.34$ meters

5. *necessary information*: <u>$20</u>, <u>$1.15</u>
    labels for proportion: $\dfrac{\$}{\text{gallons}}$
    $\dfrac{\$20}{n} = \dfrac{\$1.15}{1 \text{ gallon}}$
    $1.15 \times n = 1 \times 20$
    $1.15n = 20$
    $n = \dfrac{20}{1.15}$
    $n = 17.39$

6. *necessary information*: <u>1.61 kilometers</u>, <u>55 miles per hour</u>

    labels for proportion:
    $\dfrac{\text{kilometers}}{\text{miles}} = \dfrac{\text{kilometers per hour}}{\text{miles per hour}}$

    (This proportion will work because the "per hour" appears on both top and bottom.)

    $\dfrac{1.61 \text{ kilometers}}{1 \text{ mile}} = \dfrac{n \text{ kilometers per hour}}{55 \text{ miles per hour}}$

    $1 \times n = 1.61 \times 55$
    $n = 88.55$ kilometers per hour

ANSWER KEY (continued)

Exercise 5

1. *necessary information:* $\frac{1}{16}$ inch, 2 inches

labels for proportion: $\frac{\text{slices}}{\text{inch}}$

$$\frac{1 \text{ slice}}{\frac{1}{16} \text{ inch}} = \frac{n \text{ slices}}{2 \text{ inches}}$$

$\frac{1}{16} \times n = 1 \times 2$

$n = 2 \div \frac{1}{16}$

$n = \frac{2}{1} \times \frac{16}{1} = 32$ slices

2. *necessary information:* $1\frac{5}{8}$ ounces, 60 Baby Ruth candy bars

labels for proportion: $\frac{\text{ounce}}{\text{Baby Ruth}}$

$$\frac{1\frac{5}{8} \text{ ounces}}{1 \text{ Baby Ruth}} = \frac{n \text{ ounces}}{60 \text{ Baby Ruth}}$$

$1 \times n = 1\frac{5}{8} \times 60$

$n = \frac{13}{\underset{2}{8}} \times \overset{15}{60} = \frac{195}{2} = 97\frac{1}{2}$ ounces

(50 Hershey chocolate bars is unnecessary information.)

3. *necessary information:* 1,460 loaves, $1\frac{3}{4}$ teaspoons

labels for proportion: $\frac{\text{teaspoons}}{\text{loaves}}$

$$\frac{1\frac{3}{4} \text{ teaspoons}}{1 \text{ loaf}} = \frac{n \text{ teaspoons}}{1,460 \text{ loaves}}$$

$1 \times n = 1\frac{3}{4} \times 1,460$

$n = \frac{7}{\underset{1}{4}} \times \overset{365}{1,460} = 2,555$ teaspoons

4. *necessary information:* $\frac{7}{8}$ inch, 35 inches

labels for proportion: $\frac{\text{inches}}{\text{books}}$

$$\frac{\frac{7}{8} \text{ inch}}{1 \text{ book}} = \frac{35 \text{ inches}}{n \text{ books}}$$

$\frac{7}{8} \times n = 1 \times 35$

$n = 35 \div \frac{7}{8}$

$n = \overset{5}{35} \times \frac{8}{\underset{1}{7}} = 40$ books

5. *necessary information:* $9\frac{2}{3}$ ounces, 16 cans

labels for proportion: $\frac{\text{cans}}{\text{ounces}}$

$$\frac{1 \text{ can}}{9\frac{2}{3} \text{ ounces}} = \frac{16 \text{ cans}}{n \text{ ounces}}$$

$1 \times n = 9\frac{2}{3} \times 16$

$n = \frac{29}{3} \times 16 = \frac{464}{3}$

$n = 154\frac{2}{3}$ ounces

6. *necessary information:* 8 cups, $\frac{1}{4}$ cup

labels for proportion: $\frac{\text{cups}}{\text{loads}}$

$$\frac{8 \text{ cups}}{n \text{ loads}} = \frac{\frac{1}{4} \text{ cup}}{1 \text{ load}}$$

$\frac{1}{4} \times n = 8$

$n = 8 \div \frac{1}{4}$

$n = 8 \times \frac{4}{1} = 32$ loads

7. *necessary information:* 160 pea pods, $\frac{1}{4}$ pound

labels for proportion: $\frac{\text{pea pods}}{\text{pound}}$

$$\frac{160 \text{ pea pods}}{1 \text{ pound}} = \frac{n \text{ pea pods}}{\frac{1}{4} \text{ pound}}$$

$1 \times n = \overset{40}{160} \times \frac{1}{\underset{1}{4}}$

$n = 40$ pea pods

Exercise 6

1. *conversion:* 12 months = 1 year

$$\frac{12 \text{ months}}{1 \text{ year}} = \frac{30 \text{ months}}{n \text{ years}}$$

$12 \times n = 1 \times 30$

$12n = 30$

$n = \frac{30}{12} = \frac{5}{2} = 2\frac{1}{2}$ years

2. *conversion:* 4 quarts = 1 gallon

$$\frac{4 \text{ quarts}}{1 \text{ gallon}} = \frac{n \text{ quarts}}{200 \text{ gallons}}$$

$1 \times n = 4 \times 200$

$n = 800$ gallons

3. *conversion:* 1,000 meters = 1 kilometer

$$\frac{1,000 \text{ meters}}{1 \text{ kilometer}} = \frac{10,000 \text{ meters}}{n \text{ kilometers}}$$

$1,000 \times n = 1 \times 10,000$

$1,000n = 10,000$

$n = \frac{10,000}{1,000} = 10$ kilometers

4. *conversion:* 2,000 pounds = 1 ton

$$\frac{2,000 \text{ pounds}}{1 \text{ ton}} = \frac{n \text{ pounds}}{\frac{1}{2} \text{ ton}}$$

$$1 \times n = \overset{1,000}{\cancel{2,000}} \times \frac{1}{\cancel{2}}$$

$$n = 1,000 \text{ pounds}$$

5. *conversion:* 32 ounces = 1 quart

$$\frac{32 \text{ ounces}}{1 \text{ quart}} = \frac{n \text{ ounces}}{3 \text{ quarts}}$$

$$1 \times n = 32 \times 3$$

$$n = 96 \text{ ounces}$$

6. *conversion:* 5,280 feet = 1 mile

$$\frac{5,280 \text{ feet}}{1 \text{ mile}} = \frac{29,028 \text{ feet}}{n \text{ miles}}$$

$$5,280 \times n = 1 \times 29,028$$

$$n = \frac{29,028}{5,280} = 5.5 \text{ miles}$$

Exercise 7

1. $\dfrac{\$12.60}{1 \text{ yard}} = \dfrac{n}{3\frac{1}{3} \text{ yards}}$

$$1 \times n = \$12.60 \times 3\frac{1}{3}$$

$$n = \overset{4.20}{\cancel{12.60}} \times \frac{10}{\cancel{3}\,1} = \$42.00$$

2. $\dfrac{13.5 \text{ pounds}}{4\frac{1}{2} \text{ years}} = \dfrac{n \text{ pounds}}{1 \text{ year}}$

$$4\frac{1}{2} \times n = 13.5 \times 1$$

$$\frac{9}{2}n = 13.5$$

$$n = 13.5 \div \frac{9}{2}$$

$$n = 13.5 \times \frac{2}{9} = \frac{27.0}{9} = 3 \text{ pounds}$$

3. $\dfrac{2\frac{2}{3} \text{ pounds}}{\$3.25} = \dfrac{1 \text{ pound}}{n}$

$$2\frac{2}{3} \times n = 3.25 \times 1$$

$$\frac{8}{3}n = 3.25$$

$$n = 3.25 \div \frac{8}{3}$$

$$n = 3.25 \times \frac{3}{8} = \frac{9.75}{8}$$

$$n = 1.218 \text{ or } \$1.22$$

4. $\dfrac{7\frac{1}{2} \text{ rolls}}{\$384.50} = \dfrac{1 \text{ roll}}{n}$

$$7\frac{1}{2} \times n = 1 \times 384.50$$

$$\frac{15}{2}n = 384.50$$

$$n = 384.50 \div \frac{15}{2}$$

$$n = 384.50 \times \frac{2}{15} = \frac{769}{15}$$

$$n = 51.266 \text{ or } \$51.27$$

Exercise 8

1. *necessary information:* $\frac{1}{12}$ of an hour, 8 hours

labels for proportion: $\dfrac{\text{chickens}}{\text{hour}}$

$$\frac{1 \text{ chicken}}{\frac{1}{12} \text{ hour}} = \frac{n \text{ chickens}}{8 \text{ hours}}$$

$$\frac{1}{12} \times n = 1 \times 8$$

$$n = 8 \div \frac{1}{12}$$

$$n = 8 \times 12$$

$$n = 96 \text{ chickens}$$

2. *necessary information:* 8 blood samples, 60 minutes

labels for proportion: $\dfrac{\text{minutes}}{\text{blood samples}}$

$$\frac{60 \text{ minutes}}{8 \text{ blood samples}} = \frac{n \text{ minutes}}{1 \text{ blood sample}}$$

$$8 \times n = 1 \times 60$$

$$n = \frac{60}{8} = \frac{15}{2}$$

$$n = 7\frac{1}{2} \text{ minutes}$$

3. *necessary information:* 1.6 kilometers, 26 miles

labels for proportion: $\dfrac{\text{kilometers}}{\text{miles}}$

$$\frac{1.6 \text{ kilometers}}{1 \text{ mile}} = \frac{n \text{ kilometers}}{26 \text{ miles}}$$

$$1 \times n = 1.6 \times 26$$

$$n = 41.6 \text{ kilometers}$$

4. *necessary information:* 6 feet, 24 hours

labels for proportion: $\dfrac{\text{feet}}{\text{hours}}$

$$\frac{6 \text{ feet}}{1 \text{ hour}} = \frac{n \text{ feet}}{24 \text{ hours}}$$

$$1 \times n = 6 \times 24$$

$$n = 144 \text{ feet}$$

5. *necessary information:* .04 ounce, 12 ounces

labels for proportion: $\dfrac{\text{grams}}{\text{ounce}}$

$$\frac{1 \text{ gram}}{.04 \text{ ounce}} = \frac{n \text{ grams}}{12 \text{ ounces}}$$

$$.04 \times n = 1 \times 12$$

$$.04n = 12$$

$$n = \frac{12}{.04}$$

$$n = 300 \text{ grams}$$

ANSWER KEY (continued)

Exercise 8 continued

6. *necessary information:* $3\frac{1}{4}$ pounds, two pumpkin pies

labels for proportion: $\dfrac{\text{pounds}}{\text{pies}}$

$$\frac{3\frac{1}{4}\ \text{pounds}}{2\ \text{pies}} = \frac{n\ \text{pounds}}{10\ \text{pies}}$$

$2 \times n = 10 \times 3\frac{1}{4}$

$2n = 10 \times \frac{13}{4}$

$2n = \frac{130}{4}$

$n = \frac{130}{4} \div 2$

$n = \frac{65\cancel{130}}{4} \times \frac{1}{\cancel{2}_1}$

$n = \frac{65}{4}$

$n = 16\frac{1}{4}$ pounds

7. *necessary information:* 68,000 gallons of water

labels for proportion: $\dfrac{\text{gallons}}{\text{hour}}$

conversion: 1 day = 24 hours

$$\frac{68,000\ \text{gallons}}{1\ \text{hour}} = \frac{n}{24\ \text{hours}}$$

$1 \times n = 68,000 \times 24$

$n = 1,632,000$ gallons

8. *necessary information:* \$.12, $4\frac{1}{4}$ feet

labels for proportion: $\dfrac{\$}{\text{feet}}$

$$\frac{\$.12}{1\ \text{foot}} = \frac{n}{4\frac{1}{4}\ \text{feet}}$$

$1 \times n = \$.12 \times 4\frac{1}{4}$

$n = \$.\cancel{12}^{.03} \times \frac{17}{\cancel{4}_1}$

$n = \$.51$

9. *necessary information:* $3\frac{1}{2}$ minutes

labels for proportion: $\dfrac{\text{seconds}}{\text{minutes}}$

$$\frac{60\ \text{seconds}}{1\ \text{minute}} = \frac{n}{3\frac{1}{2}\ \text{minutes}}$$

$1 \times n = 60 \times 3\frac{1}{2}$

$n = {}^{30}\cancel{60} \times \frac{7}{\cancel{2}_1}$

$n = 210$ seconds

10. *necessary information:* 942 pages, 302,382 words

labels for proportion: $\dfrac{\text{words}}{\text{pages}}$

$$\frac{302,382\ \text{words}}{942\ \text{pages}} = \frac{n}{1\ \text{page}}$$

$942 \times n = 1 \times 302,382$

$942n = 302,382$

$n = \dfrac{302,382}{942}$

$n = 321$ words

CHAPTER 8

Exercise 1

1. multiplication
2. addition
3. division
4. subtraction
5. multiplication
6. subtraction
7. addition
8 division

Exercise 2

1. e.
current year − age = birth year
1983 − 86 = 1897
(Married 51 years is unneccessary information.)

2. e.
rent per roommate × roommates = total rent
\$140 × 4 roommates = \$560

3. d.
cars per trip × number of trips = total cars
35 cars × 7 trips = 245 cars

4. b.
old population + rise = new population
596,640 people + 37,290 people = 633,930 people

5. a.
$\dfrac{\text{watts}}{\text{lights}} = \dfrac{\text{watts}}{\text{lights}}$

$\dfrac{2}{1} = \dfrac{300}{n}$

$2n = 300$

$n = \dfrac{300}{2} = 150$ lights

6. c.
$\dfrac{\text{cables}}{\text{calls}} = \dfrac{\text{cables}}{\text{calls}}$

$\dfrac{1}{12,500} = \dfrac{n}{87,500}$

$12,500\,n = 87,500$

$n = \dfrac{87,500}{12,500} = 7$ cables

7. e.
amount paid + tax = total amount
\$360 + \$18 = \$378

8. a.
total cloth ÷ number of looms = cloth per loom
8,760 yards ÷ 60 looms = 146 yards of cloth

9. b.
top month's sales − goal = extra sales
37 encyclopedias − 20 encyclopedias = 17 encyclopedias

10. d.
number of ears × kernels per ear = total kernels
91,035 ears × 315 kernels per ear = 28,676,025 kernels

Exercise 3

1. b.

total bill − tax = cost of sandwich alone
$1.89 − $.09 = $1.80

2. a.

Soviet Union − United States = difference
231,300,845 people − 213,478,921 people = 17,821,924 people

3. d.

string ÷ length of pieces = number of pieces
12 foot ÷ $\frac{3}{4}$ foot piece = 16 pieces

4. b.

cost of repair − amount deductible = insurance payment
$1,125 − $250 = $875

5. d.

total amount for chicken ÷ price per pound = weight of chicken
$2.90 ÷ $.65 = 4.46 lbs.

6. b.

$$\frac{\frac{1}{250} \text{ second}}{1 \text{ time}} = \frac{5 \text{ seconds}}{n \text{ times}}$$

$$\frac{1}{250} \times n = 5 \times 1$$

$$n = 5 \times \frac{250}{1} = 1,250 \text{ times}$$

7. e.

$$\frac{\frac{5}{8} \text{ ounce}}{1 \text{ bottle}} = \frac{16 \text{ ounces}}{n \text{ bottles}}$$

$$\frac{5}{8} \times n = 1 \times 16$$

$$n = 16 \times \frac{8}{5} = \frac{128}{5} = 25\frac{3}{5} \text{ bottles}$$

Amanda filled $25\frac{3}{5}$ bottles; therefore, she used 26 bottles.

($3\frac{1}{2}$ inches high is unnecessary information.)

8. c.

miles ÷ hours = average speed
3,855 ÷ $3\frac{3}{4}$ hours = 1,028 miles per hour

9. a.

fraction (of) × paycheck = food cost
$\frac{1}{3} \times $174 = 58
($\frac{1}{4}$ of her paycheck is not necessary information.)

10. c.

teachers + aides = total people
216 teachers + 85 aides = 301 people

11. b.

normal depth + above normal = total depth
7 feet + 14 feet = 21 feet

12. d.

$$\frac{1 \text{ stick}}{\frac{1}{4} \text{ pound}} = \frac{\frac{1}{2} \text{ stick}}{n \text{ pound}}$$

$$1 \times n = \frac{1}{4} \times \frac{1}{2} = \frac{1}{8} \text{ pound}$$

13. e.

original − thickness needed = amount sanded
$\frac{7}{8}$ inch − $\frac{13}{16}$ inch = $\frac{1}{16}$ inch

14. d.

price per pound × pounds = amount paid
$1.16 × 3.6 pounds = $4.18 paid

15. a.

total needed − amount raised = amount to be raised
$\frac{2}{3}$ of expenses − $\frac{4}{9}$ of expenses = $\frac{2}{9}$ of expenses

16. b.

weight of girder × girders = amount of steel
4 tons × 1,200 girders = 4,800 tons of steel

17. a.

miles ÷ gallons = miles per gallon
283.1 miles ÷ 14.9 gallons = 19 miles per gallon

18. c.

Harry + Fran = total floor sanded
$\frac{1}{6}$ of the floor + $\frac{1}{4}$ of the floor = $\frac{5}{12}$ of the floor

19. c.

fraction (of) × total recipe = flour needed
$\frac{1}{2} \times 3$ cups = $1\frac{1}{2}$ cups

20. a.

newspapers × cost = total cost
304 newspapers × $.35 = $106.40

21. e.

heavier − lighter = difference
2.2 pounds − 1.84 pounds = .36 pound

22. c.

peaches + plums = total weight
1.72 pounds + .9 pound = 2.62 pounds

23. b.

stock closing − stock opening = gain
$22\frac{1}{2} − 20\frac{3}{8} = 2\frac{1}{8}$

24. d.

deposit × weeks = total money
$28 × 52 weeks = $1,456

CHAPTER 9

Exercise 1

1. percent
2. part
3. whole
4. part
5. whole
6. percent
7. part
8. percent
9. part
10. whole

ANSWER KEY (continued)

Exercise 2

1. *part:* 36
whole: 144
percent: n (is what %?)

$$\frac{36}{144} = \frac{n}{100}$$

$144 \times n = 36 \times 100$

$144n = 3,600$

$$n = \frac{3,600}{144}$$

$n = 25\%$

2. *part:* 288
percent: 72%
whole: n (of what number?)

$$\frac{288}{n} = \frac{72}{100}$$

$72 \times n = 100 \times 288$

$72n = 28,800$

$$n = \frac{28,800}{72}$$

$n = 400$

3. *whole:* 75
percent: 68%
part: n (What is?)

$$\frac{n}{75} = \frac{68}{100}$$

$100 \times n = 75 \times 68$

$100n = 5,100$

$$n = \frac{5,100}{100}$$

$n = 51$

4. *whole:* $160
part: $40
percent: n (What was the percent?)

$$\frac{40}{160} = \frac{n}{100}$$

$160 \times n = 40 \times 100$

$160n = 4,000$

$$n = \frac{4,000}{160}$$

$n = 25\%$

5. *percent:* 58%
whole: 28,450 votes
part: n (How many votes did she receive?)

$$\frac{n}{28,450} = \frac{58}{100}$$

$100 \times n = 58 \times 28,450$

$100n = 1,650,100$

$$n = \frac{1,650,100}{100}$$

$n = 16,501$ votes

6. *percent:* 25%
part: $96,000
whole: n (How much aid was Metropolis receiving?)

$$\frac{96,000}{n} = \frac{25}{100}$$

$25 \times n = 96,000 \times 100$

$25n = 9,600,000$

$$n = \frac{9,600,000}{25}$$

$n = \$384,000$

7. *percent:* 7%
part: $553
whole: n (What was his income?)

$$\frac{553}{n} = \frac{7}{100}$$

$7 \times n = 553 \times 100$

$7n = 55,300$

$$n = \frac{55,300}{7}$$

$n = \$7,900$

8. *percent:* 60%
whole: 345,780
part: n (How many black people live in the city?)

$$\frac{n}{345,780} = \frac{60}{100}$$

$100 \times n = 345,780 \times 60$

$100n = 20,746,800$

$$n = \frac{20,746,800}{100}$$

$n = 207,468$ black people

9. *part:* $340
whole: $2,000
percent: n (What was the interest rate?)

$$\frac{340}{2,000} = \frac{n}{100}$$

$2,000 \times n = 340 \times 100$

$2,000n = 34,000$

$$n = \frac{34,000}{2,000}$$

$n = 17\%$

Exercise 3

1. *percent:* 4.5%
part: 90
whole: n (of what number?)

$$\frac{90}{n} = \frac{4.5}{100}$$

$4.5 \times n = 90 \times 100$

$4.5n = 9,000$

$$n = \frac{9,000}{4.5}$$

$n = 2,000$

2. *part:* $\frac{1}{10}$

whole: $\frac{3}{4}$

percent: n (is what percent?)

$$\frac{\frac{1}{10}}{\frac{3}{4}} = \frac{n}{100}$$

$$\frac{3}{4} \times n = 100 \times \frac{1}{10}$$

$$\frac{3}{4}n = 10$$

$$n = 10 \div \frac{3}{4}$$

$$n = 10 \times \frac{4}{3} = \frac{40}{3} = 13\frac{1}{3}$$

$$n = 13\frac{1}{3}\%$$

3. *percent:* $66\frac{2}{3}\%$

part: 42

whole: n (of what number?)

$$\frac{42}{n} = \frac{66\frac{2}{3}}{100}$$

$$66\frac{2}{3} \times n = 42 \times 100$$

$$66\frac{2}{3}n = 4,200$$

$$\frac{200n}{3} = 4,200$$

$$n = \overset{21}{4,200} \times \frac{3}{\underset{1}{200}} = 63$$

$$n = 63$$

4. *percent:* 6.4%

whole: 800

part: n (what is?)

$$\frac{n}{800} = \frac{6.4}{100}$$

$$100 \times n = 6.4 \times 800$$

$$100n = 5,120$$

$$n = \frac{5,120}{100}$$

$$n = 51.2$$

5. *percent:* 8%

part: $49.76

whole: n (How much money?)

$$\frac{49.76}{n} = \frac{8}{100}$$

$$8 \times n = 49.76 \times 100$$

$$8n = 4,976$$

$$n = \frac{4,976}{8}$$

$$n = \$622$$

6. *whole:* $8.60

percent: 5%

part: n (How much was the tax?)

$$\frac{n}{8.60} = \frac{5}{100}$$

$$100 \times n = 8.60 \times 5$$

$$100n = 43$$

$$n = \frac{43}{100}$$

$$n = \$.43$$

7. *part:* $.96

whole: $1.92

percent: n (By what percent?)

$$\frac{.96}{1.92} = \frac{n}{100}$$

$$1.92 \times n = .96 \times 100$$

$$1.92n = 96$$

$$n = \frac{96}{1.92}$$

$$n = 50\%$$

8. *whole:* $12.80

percent: $12\frac{1}{2}\%$

part: n (How much did Juan save?)

$$\frac{n}{12.80} = \frac{12\frac{1}{2}}{100}$$

$$100 \times n = 12.80 \times 12\frac{1}{2}$$

$$100n = \overset{6.40}{12.80} \times \frac{25}{\underset{2}{4}}$$

$$100n = 160$$

$$n = \frac{160}{100}$$

$$n = \$1.60$$

Exercise 4

1. *part:* 3 out of

whole: 4 dentists

percent: n (What percent of all dentists?)

$$\frac{3}{4} = \frac{n}{100}$$

$$4 \times n = 3 \times 100$$

$$4n = 300$$

$$n = \frac{300}{4} = 75\%$$

2. *percent:* 40%

part: 112,492 people

whole: n (How many registered voters?)

$$\frac{112,492}{n} = \frac{40}{100}$$

$$40 \times n = 112,492 \times 100$$

$$40n = 11,249,200$$

$$n = \frac{11,249,200}{40} = 281,230 \text{ people}$$

3. *part:* 11,500 fewer visitors

whole: 34,500 visitors

percent: n (What was the percent drop?)

$$\frac{11,500}{34,500} = \frac{n}{100}$$

$$34,500 \times n = 11,500 \times 100$$

$$34,500n = 1,150,000$$

$$n = \frac{1,150,000}{34,500} = 33\frac{1}{3}\%$$

ANSWER KEY (continued)

Exercise 4 continued
---

4. *whole:* $49,600,000
percent: 8.6%
part: n (How much money did the company make?)

$$\frac{n}{49,600,000} = \frac{8.6}{100}$$

$100 \times n = 8.6 \times 49,600,000$
$100n = 426,560,000$
$n = \frac{426,560,000}{100} = \$4,265,600$

5. *part:* .4 ounce
percent: $16\frac{2}{3}$%
whole: n (What was the weight of its chocolate bar before the change?)

$$\frac{.4}{n} = \frac{16\frac{2}{3}}{100}$$

$16\frac{2}{3} \times n = 100 \times .4$
$16\frac{2}{3}n = 40$
$\frac{50}{3}n = 40$
$n = 40 \div \frac{50}{3}$
$n = \overset{4}{\cancel{40}} \times \frac{3}{\underset{5}{\cancel{50}}} = 4 \times \frac{3}{5} =$
$\frac{12}{5} = 2\frac{2}{5}$ or 2.4 ounces

6. *part:* 40
percent: .8%
whole: n (How many people over age 65?)
$$\frac{40}{n} = \frac{.8}{100}$$
$.8 \times n = 40 \times 100$
$.8n = 4,000$
$n = \frac{4,000}{.8} = 5,000$ people over age 65

7. *percent:* 13%
whole: $11,694
part: n (How much did he pay?)

$$\frac{n}{11,694} = \frac{13}{100}$$

$100 \times n = 13 \times 11,694$
$100n = 152,022$
$n = \frac{152,022}{100} = \$1,520.22$

8. *whole:* $17,548
percent: 7%
part: n (How much of a raise will he get?)

$$\frac{n}{17,548} = \frac{7}{100}$$

$100 \times n = 17,548 \times 7$
$100n = 122,836$
$n = \frac{122,836}{100} = \$1,228.36$

9. *part:* $18
percent: 9%
whole: n (What was her week's salary?)

$$\frac{18}{n} = \frac{9}{100}$$

$9 \times n = 18 \times 100$
$9n = 1,800$
$n = \frac{1,800}{9} = \$200$

10. *part:* 506
whole: 1,012 attempts
percent: n (What was his scoring percentage?)

$$\frac{506}{1,012} = \frac{n}{100}$$

$1,012 \times n = 506 \times 100$
$1,012n = 50,600$
$n = \frac{50,600}{1,012} = 50\%$

CHAPTER 10

Exercise 1

Information given in the problem is written under the appropriate place in the word sentence or proportion. Your wording may differ slightly.

1. *solution sentence:*
earnings − *money taken out* = take-home pay
   ($230)

missing information:
taxes + *union dues* = *money taken out*
 ($49)   ($6)

2. *solution sentence:*
starting money − *money spent* = ending money
   ($41)

missing information:
lunch + *gas* = *money spent*
 ($3)   ($22)

3. *solution sentence:*
starting balance + *transactions* = new
       ($394)
balance

missing information:
deposit − *check* = *transactions*
 ($201)   ($187)

4. *solution sentence:*
cost of blouses + cost of skirt = total spent
(\$16)

missing information:
cost per blouse × *number of blouses* = *cost of blouses*
(\$12)$$(5)

5. *solution sentence:*
total amount ÷ monthly payments = amount
of each payment (24)

missing information:
loan + *interest* = *total amount to pay*
(\$4,600)(\$728)

6. *solution sentence:*
total cost ÷ *number of dolls* = cost per doll
(\$720)

missing information:
boxes × *dolls per box* = *number of dolls*
(30)(8)

7. *proportion:*
(5)$$(30)
$$\frac{\text{cost}}{\text{pieces}} = \frac{\text{total cost}}{\text{pieces able to buy}}$$
(3)

8. *solution sentence:*
amount paid − *price of clothes* = change
(100)

missing information:
skirt + *blouse* = *price of clothes*
(\$14)(\$9)

9. *proportion:*
(10,000)
$$\frac{\text{numbers entered}}{\text{minutes}} = \frac{\text{numbers entered}}{\text{minutes}}$$
(60)$$(15)

10. *solution sentence:*
room area × number of rooms = total carpet
(3)

missing information:
length × *width* = *room area*
(20)(15)

Exercise 2

1. *solution sentence:*
ward delegates + at large = total delegates
ward delegates + 5 = total delegates

missing information:
wards × *delegates* = *ward delegates*
8 × 4 = *32 ward delegates*

solution:
32 + 5 = 37 delegates

2. *solution sentence:*
customer price − cost = profit
163 − *cost* = profit

missing information:
parts + *labor* = *cost*
81 + *45* = *\$126 cost*

solution:
163 − *126* = \$37 profit

3. $\dfrac{\text{copies}}{\text{minutes}} = \dfrac{n \text{ copies}}{\text{minutes}}$

$\dfrac{30}{5} = \dfrac{n}{60}$

$5 \times n = 30 \times 60$

$5n = 1{,}800$

$n = \dfrac{1{,}800}{5} = 360$ copies

4. *solution sentence:*
driving cost + other costs = Jennifer's
spending
driving cost + 114 = Jennifer's

missing information:
total money ÷ *people* = *driving cost*
216 ÷ *4* = *\$54 driving cost*

solution:
54 + 114 = \$168

5. *solution sentence:*
total people ÷ people per bus = total buses
total people ÷ *40* = total buses

missing information:
union members + *other people* = *total people*
4,168 + *1,272* = *5,440 total people*

solution:
5,440 ÷ *40* = 136 buses

6. *solution sentence:*
raise − new expenses = monthly net increase
78 − *new expenses* = monthly net increase

missing information:
daily increase × *number of days* = *new*
expenses
2 × *22* = *\$44 new expenses*

solution:
78 − *44* = \$34 monthly net increase

7. $\dfrac{\text{people}}{\text{pounds}} = \dfrac{\text{people}}{\text{pounds}}$

$\dfrac{6}{3} = \dfrac{8}{n}$

$6 \times n = 3 \times 8$

$6n = 24$

$n = \dfrac{24}{6} = 4$ pounds

ANSWER KEY (continued)

Exercise 2 continued

8. *solution sentence:*
total votes − 2 candidates' votes = other candidate votes
7,481 − 2 candidates' votes = other candidate votes

missing information:
Carter + Reagan = 2 candidates' votes
2,896 + 4,201 = 7,097 votes

solution:
7,481 − 7,097 = 384 votes

Exercise 3

1. *solution sentence:*
total cost ÷ total cookies = cost per cookie
14.40 ÷ total cookies = cost per cookie

missing information:
cookies × number of boxes = total cookies
20 × 6 = 120 cookies

solution:
14.40 ÷ 120 = $.12 cost per cookie

2. *solution sentence:*
original price − reduction = sale price
400 − reduction = sale price

missing information:
original price × percent = reduction
400 × .30 = $120.00

solution:
400 − 120 = $280 sale price

3. *solution sentence:*
pears + fruit cocktail = total fruit
pears + $17\frac{1}{2}$ = total fruit

missing information:
cans × contents = ounces pears
5 × $9\frac{3}{4}$ = $48\frac{3}{4}$ ounces

solution:
$48\frac{3}{4}$ + $17\frac{1}{2}$ = $66\frac{1}{4}$ ounces

4. *solution sentence:*
total saving − cost = net saving
total saving − 2.49 = net saving

missing information:
saving × months = total saving
3.40 × 12 = $40.80

solution:
40.80 − 2.49 = $38.31 net saving

5. *solution sentence:*
original weight − *loss* = cooked weight
$\frac{1}{4}$ pound − *loss* = cooked weight

missing information:
weight × fraction = loss
$\frac{1}{4}$ × $\frac{1}{3}$ = $\frac{1}{12}$ *loss*

solution:
$\frac{1}{4}$ − $\frac{1}{12}$ = $\frac{1}{6}$ pound

6. *solution sentence:*
dinner + tax = total cost
24 + tax = total cost

missing information:
dinner × percent = tax
24 × .06 = $1.44

solution:
24 + 1.44 = $25.44 total

7. *solution sentence:*
original price − discount = sale price
19.50 − discount = sale price

missing information:
price × percent = discount
19.50 × .30 = $5.85 discount

solution:
19.50 − 5.85 = $13.65

8. *solution sentence:*
payment ÷ months = monthly payment
payment ÷ 12 = monthly payment

missing information:
amount − down payment = payment
310.60 − 130 = $180.60

solution:
180.60 ÷ 12 = $15.05 monthly payment

9. *solution sentence:*
price per bottle − cost per bottle = profit per bottle
2.10 − cost per bottle = profit per bottle

missing information:
cost ÷ bottles = cost per bottle
57 ÷ 30 = $1.90

solution:
2.10 − 1.90 = $.20 profit

10. *proportion:*
$$\frac{part}{whole} = \frac{percent}{100}$$
$$\frac{profit}{57} = \frac{n\ percent}{100}$$
missing information:
bottles × cost = profit
30 × .20 = $6

solution:

$$\frac{6}{57} = \frac{n}{100}$$

$$57 \times n = 6 \times 100$$

$$57n = 600$$

$$n = \frac{600}{57} = 10.5\%$$

Exercise 4:

1. floor size ÷ tile size = number of tiles
    floor size ÷ 81 = number of tiles
    conversion:
    (144 square inches in a square foot)
    $$\frac{square\ inches}{1\ square\ foot} = \frac{n\ square\ inches}{square\ feet}$$
    $$\frac{144}{1} = \frac{n}{54}$$
    n = 144 × 54 = 7,776 square inches
    solution:
    7,776 ÷ 81 = 96 tiles

2. welds per hour × hours = total welds
    20 × 9 = 180 total welds

3. highway ÷ reflector distance = number of
    reflectors
    highway ÷ 528 = reflectors
    conversion: (1 mile = 5,280 feet)
    $$\frac{feet}{mile} = \frac{feet}{mile}$$
    $$\frac{5,280}{1} = \frac{n}{46}$$
    n = 242,880 feet
    solution:
    242,880 ÷ 528 = 460 reflectors

    (Another acceptable answer would be 461
    reflectors. This would depend on whether the first
    or the second reflector was at the first 528-foot
    mark.)

4. gallons needed × pints per gallon = total
    people
    gallons × 8 = total people
    (There are 8 pints in a gallon.)
    missing information:
    gallons − donations = gallons needed
    48 − 26 = 22 gallons needed
    solution:
    22 × 8 = 176 people

5. total coal ÷ pounds per customer = customers
    total coal ÷ 400 = customers
    conversion: (There are 2,000 pounds in a ton.)
    $$\frac{pounds}{1\ ton} = \frac{pounds}{ton}$$
    $$\frac{2,000}{1} = \frac{n}{38}$$
    n = 76,000 pounds

solution:
76,000 ÷ 400 = 190 customers

6. $$\frac{numbers}{time} = \frac{numbers}{time}$$
    $$\frac{463}{5} = \frac{n}{60}$$
    (There are 60 minutes in an hour.)
    5n = 27,780
    $$n = \frac{27,780}{5} = 5,556\ numbers$$

7. ice cream: ÷ serving = number of people
    ice cream ÷ 4 = number of people
    conversion: (1 quart contains 32 ounces.)
    $$\frac{quarts}{ounces} = \frac{quarts}{ounces}$$
    $$\frac{1}{32} = \frac{12}{n}$$
    n = 384 ounces
    solution:
    384 ÷ 4 = 96 people

Exercise 5:

1. *necessary information:* 103,912 students, 4,657
    students, 1,288 students
    original students − change = new total

    103,912 − *change* = new total
    missing information:
    left − enrolled = change
    4,657 − 1,288 = 3,369 students
    solution:
    103,912 − 3,369 = 100,543 students

2. *necessary information:* 103,912 students, 1,288
    students
    (Knowing the number of students who left the
    system is not needed to answer the question.)
    original + new enrollees = total students
    103,912 + 1,288 = 105,200 students

3. *necessary information:* 54 degrees, 27 degrees, 19
    degrees
    high temperature − drop = midnight
    temperature
    high temperature − 19 = midnight temperature
    missing information:
    first + rise = high temperature
    54 + 27 = 81 degree high
    solution:
    81 − 19 = 62 degrees midnight temperature

4. *necessary information:* $148, 52 weeks
    (The amount of money taken out is not necessary
    information.)
    weekly income × number of weeks = yearly
    148 × 52 = $7,696

ANSWER KEY (continued)

Exercise 5 continued

5. *necessary information:* 3 paperbacks, $2.95, 10-dollar bill

    (The information about magazines is not necessary information.)

    money paid − cost of books = change

    10.00 − *cost of books* = change

    missing information:
    books × price = cost of books
    2.95 × 3 = $8.85

    solution:
    10.00 − 8.85 = $1.15 change

6. *necessary information:* 20%, $1.65

    (The weight of the oranges is not needed to answer the question.)

    cost − amount of discount = final price

    1.65 − *amount of discount* = final price

    missing information:
    cost × percent = amount of discount
    1.65 × .20 = $.33

    solution:
    1.65 − .33 = $1.32 final price

Exercise 6

1. apples + cantaloupe = total

    apples + .88 = total

    missing information:

    $$\frac{cost}{apples} = \frac{cost}{apples}$$
    $$\frac{1.56}{12} = \frac{n}{7}$$
    $$12n = 10.92$$
    $$n = 10.92 \div 12 = \$.91$$

    solution:
    .91 + .88 = $1.79

2. bill − discount = new bill

    36.80 − *discount* = new bill

    missing information:
    bill × percent = discount
    36.80 × .06 = 2.208 = $2.21

    solution:
    36.80 − 2.21 = $34.59

3. reduced calories − breakfast = rest of day

    reduced calories − 797 = rest of day

    missing information:
    original − (percent × calories) = reduced calories
    4,200 − (.28 × 4,200) = reduced calories
    4,200 − 1,176 = 3,024 calories

    solution:
    3,024 − 797 = 2,227 calories

4. salary + commission = pay

    70 + *commission* = pay

    missing information:
    percent × sales over 200 = commission
    .06 × (1,160 − 200) = commission
    .06 × 960 = $57.60

    solution:
    70 + 57.60 = $127.60

5. money spent ÷ gallons = price per gallon

    186 ÷ *gallons* = price per gallon

    missing information:
    miles ÷ miles per gallon = gallons
    3,627 ÷ 31 = 117 gallons

    solution:
    186 ÷ 117 = 1.589 *or* $1.59 per gallon

Exercise 7

1. c.
    daily miles × days = total miles
    daily miles × 5 = total

    missing information:
    to work + back + delivery = daily miles
    7 + 7 + 296 = 310 miles

    solution:
    310 × 5 = 1,550 miles

2. a.
    miles travel + miles at work = daily miles
    14 + 296 = 310 miles

    (5 days a week is unnecessary information.)

3. c.
    total ÷ students = individual cost
    total ÷ 15 = individual cost

    missing information:
    books + materials = total
    135 + 225 = $360

    solution:
    360 ÷ 15 = $24 individual

4. e.
    small rooms' capacities + main room capacity = total capacity
    small rooms' capacities + 94 = total capacity

    missing information:
    rooms × capacity = small rooms' capacities
    4 × 28 = 112 people

    solution:
    112 + 94 = 206 people

5. b.
    players × teams = players before change
    36 × 8 = 288 players before change

    (It is not necessary to know the decrease to find "players before change.")

6. **d.**

players on new rosters × teams = total after change

players on new rosters × 8 = total after change

missing information:

players − reduction = players on new rosters

36 − 3 = 33 players

solution:

33 × 8 = 264 players

7. **d.**

cheese cost + apples cost = total cost

missing information:

pounds × cost = cheese cost

2.36 × 1.58 = $3.7288 or $3.73

pounds × cost = apples cost

4 × .49 = $1.96

solution:

3.73 + 1.96 = $5.69

8. **c.**

front loading − top loading = additional loads

missing information:

cups ÷ amount = front loading

$6 ÷ \frac{1}{4} = 6 × 4 = 24$ loads

cups ÷ amount = top loading

$6 ÷ \frac{1}{3} = 6 × 3 = 18$ loads

solution:

24 − 18 = 6 loads

9. **b.**

weekly × number of weeks = yearly pay

90 × 52 = $4,680

(There are 52 weeks in a year.)

10. **e.**

pencils in a box × boxes = total pencils

pencils in a box × 17 = total pencils

missing information:

pencils in package × packages in box = pencils in a box

12 × 60 = 720 pencils

solution:

720 × 17 = 12,240 pencils

CHAPTER 11

Word Problem Review

1. **d.**

$$\frac{\text{cocoa}}{\text{chocolate}} = \frac{\text{cocoa}}{\text{chocolate}}$$

$$\frac{3 \text{ tablespoons}}{1 \text{ ounce}} = \frac{n \text{ tablespoons}}{12 \text{ ounces}}$$

$1 × n = 3 × 12 = 36$ tablespoons

(1 tablespoon fat is unnecessary information.)

2. **a.**

$$\frac{\text{liquid}}{\text{corn syrup}} = \frac{\text{liquid}}{\text{corn syrup}}$$

$$\frac{\frac{1}{4} \text{ cup liquid}}{1 \text{ cup corn syrup}} = \frac{n \text{ cup liquid}}{1\frac{1}{2} \text{ cups corn syrup}}$$

$1 × n = \frac{1}{4} × 1\frac{1}{2}$

$n = \frac{1}{4} × \frac{3}{2} = \frac{3}{8}$ cup

3. **c.**

$$\frac{\text{part}}{\text{whole}} = \frac{\text{percent}}{100}$$

$$\frac{25 \text{ square inch}}{400 \text{ square inch}} = \frac{n\%}{100}$$

$400 × n = 25 × 100$

$n = \frac{2,500}{400} = 6\frac{1}{4}\%$

4. **d.**

$$\frac{\text{pounds}}{\text{bushel}} = \frac{\text{pounds}}{\text{bushel}}$$

$$\frac{48 \text{ pounds}}{1 \text{ bushel}} = \frac{12 \text{ pounds}}{n \text{ bushels}}$$

$48 × n = 1 × 12$

$n = 12 ÷ 48 = \frac{1}{4}$ bushel

5. **c.**

$$\frac{\text{concrete}}{\text{square feet}} = \frac{\text{concrete}}{\text{square feet}}$$

$$\frac{1.23 \text{ cubic yards}}{100 \text{ square feet}} = \frac{n \text{ cubic yards}}{550 \text{ square feet}}$$

$100 × n = 1.23 × 550$

$n = 676.50 ÷ 100 = 6.765$ cubic yards

(4 inches of concrete is not necessary information.)

6. **c.**

conversion: (1 dozen eggs = 12 eggs)

$$\frac{1\frac{1}{2} \text{ pounds}}{12 \text{ eggs}} = \frac{n \text{ pounds}}{8 \text{ eggs}}$$

$12 × n = 1\frac{1}{2} × 8$

$n = \frac{3}{2} × 8 × \frac{1}{12} = \frac{24}{24} = 1$ pound

7. **b.**

total bill − air conditioning = bill without air conditioner

$86.29 − $59 = $27.29

ANSWER KEY (continued)

Word Problem Review continued

8. **a.**

$$\frac{part}{whole} = \frac{percent}{100}$$

missing information: $80\% - 70\% = 10\%$

$$\frac{n}{\$18,657} = \frac{10}{100}$$

$100 \times n = 10 \times \$18,657$
$n = 186,570 \div 100 = \$1,865.70$

9. **d.**

original gallons − *gallons delivered* = gallons left

missing information:
deliveries × gallons per delivery = gallons delivered
7 deliveries × 364 gallons = 2,548 gallons delivered
9,008 gallons − *2,548 gallons* = 6,460 gallons left

10. **a.**

charge per member × number of members = total collected

missing information:
dues + magazine = charge per member
$10 + $5 = $15
$15 × 13,819 members = $207,285

11. **a.**

P. original + N.Y. original + G. original = total value
$1,343 + $658 + $3.98 = $2,004.98

12. **e.**

original value − *value lost* = 5 year value
missing information:
$\frac{1}{3}$ *original value* + $\frac{1}{4}$ *original value = value lost*
$\frac{1}{3} \times 3,600 + \frac{1}{4} \times 3,600 = value lost$
1,200 + 900 = $2,100
3,600 − 2,100 = $1,500

13. **c.**

original cost per tool set − price of last set = money lost on last set
missing information:
total cost for sets ÷ number of sets = original cost per tool set
$540.60 ÷ 15 tool sets = $36.04
$36.04 − $24 = $12.04

14. **b.**

total weekly earnings × number of weeks = gross yearly earnings
missing information:
money taken out + take home pay = total weekly earnings
$48.23 + $132.77 = $181
$181 × 52 weeks = $9,412

15. **a.**

total tablets − *tablets taken* = tablets left
missing information:
tablets per day × number of days = tablets taken
4 tablets per day × 30 days = 120 tablets taken
250 tablets − *120 tablets* = 130 tablets

16. **b.**

total aid ÷ number of students = aid per student
missing information:
last year's aid − decrease = total aid
$1,126,200 − $462,000 = $664,200
$664,200 ÷ 820 students = $810

17. **b.**

profit ÷ number of women = profit per woman
missing information:
earnings − expenses = profit
$36,460 − $23,188 = $13,272
$13,272 ÷ 4 women = $3,318

18. **b.**

$$\frac{168 \text{ miles}}{5.6 \text{ gallons}} = \frac{417 \text{ miles}}{n \text{ gallons}}$$

$168 \times n = 5.6 \times 417$
$n = 2,335.2 \div 168 = 13.9$ gallons

19. **d.**

$$\frac{5 \text{ tablespoons}}{2 \text{ cups}} = \frac{n \text{ tablespoons}}{24 \text{ cups}}$$

$2 \times n = 5 \times 24$
$n = 120 \div 2 = 60$ tablespoons

20. **e.**

total weight ÷ weight per book = number of books
34.2 pounds ÷ .6 pound = 57 books

21. **b.**

total children − children not in public school = children in public school
5,372 children − 1,547 children = 3,825 children

22. a.

closed stations + remaining stations = last year's stations

423 stations + 2,135 stations = 2,558 service stations

23. c.

feet in a mile × number of miles = total number of feet

missing information:

feet in a yard × yards in a mile = feet in a mile

3 feet × 1,760 yards = 5,280 feet

5,280 feet × 5 miles = 26,400 feet

24. c.

weekend's hot dogs − Saturday's = Sunday's hot dogs

426 hot dogs − 198 hot dogs = 228 hot dogs

25. b.

original price − *reduction* = sale price

missing information:

fraction × original price = reduction

$\frac{1}{3} \times \$96 = \$32$

$96 − $32 = $64

26. d.

sale price + reduction = original price

$95 + $47 = $142

27. c. $148

original amount + *change* = new amount

missing information:

deposit − check = change

$115 − $28 = $87

$61 + $87 = $148

28. c.

original weight − weight loss = new weight

$172\frac{1}{2}$ pounds − $47\frac{3}{4}$ pounds = $124\frac{3}{4}$ pounds

29. d.

original weight + first month + second month = new weight

104 pounds + 3 pounds + 4 pounds = 111 pounds

30. d.

$$\frac{n \text{ undecided}}{\text{total people}} = \frac{\text{percent undecided}}{100\%}$$

missing information:

100% in favor − (in favor + against) = percent undecided

100% − (68% + 25%) = 7%

$$\frac{n}{1,400 \text{ people}} = \frac{7}{100}$$

100 × n = 7 × 1,400

100 n = 9,800

n = 98 people

31. b.

original balance − *total checks* + deposit = new balance

missing information:

first check + second check = total checks

$46.19 + $22.45 = $68.64

$74.81 − $68.64 + $60.00 = $66.17

32. d.

cost of socks + cost of towels = total spent

cost per sock × number of socks = cost of socks

$1.79 × 3 socks = $5.37

cost per towel × number of towels = cost of towels

$2.69 × 4 towels = $10.76

$5.37 + $10.76 = $16.13

33. b.

dinner + movie + babysitter = cost of evening

$14.43 + $3.50 + $5.00 = $22.93

34. b.

passengers per jet × number of jets = total passengers

214 passengers × 96 jets = 20,544 passengers

35. e.

total price − rebate = total paid

missing information:

list price + added options = total price

$6,578 + $435 = $7,013

$7,013 − $650 = $6,363

36. a.

$$\frac{\text{field goals}}{\text{field goal attempts}} = \frac{\text{scoring percentage}}{100\%}$$

missing information:

field goal attempts − misses = field goals

25 field goal attempts − 7 misses = 18 field goals

$$\frac{18 \text{ field goals}}{25 \text{ field goal attempts}} = \frac{n}{100}$$

25 × n = 18 × 100

n = 1,800 ÷ 25 = 72%

37. c.

$$\frac{432 \text{ male workers}}{\text{total work force}} = \frac{\text{percent male workers}}{100\%}$$

missing information:

100% workforce − percent female = percent male

100% − 28% = 72% male

$$\frac{432}{n} = \frac{72}{100}$$

72 × n = 432 × 100

n = 43,200 ÷ 72 = 600 workers

ANSWER KEY (continued)

Word Problem Review continued

38. b.

weight per Chevrolet × number of Chevrolets = total weight

1,600 pounds × 840 Chevrolets = 1,344,000 pounds

39. c.

weight of carton ÷ number of nails = weight per nail

$\frac{3}{4}$ pound ÷ 75 nails = $\frac{3}{4} \times \frac{1}{75} = \frac{1}{100}$ pound = .01 pound

40. b.

total cost per girl × number of girls = total collected

missing information:

cost to get in + cost of skates = cost per girl

$.75 + $.50 = $1.25

$1.25 × 19 girls = $23.75

41. d.

conversion: (1 dozen = 12 oranges)

$$\frac{\$1.50}{12 \text{ oranges}} = \frac{\$n}{4 \text{ oranges}}$$

$12 \times n = 1.50 \times 4$

$n = 6.00 \div 12 = \$.50$

42. a.

fraction (of) × total representatives = votes

$\frac{2}{3} \times 435 = 290$ votes

43. c.

total homes ÷ number of people = homes per person

948 homes ÷ 12 people = 79 homes

44. c.

$$\frac{\$684}{\$3,600} = \frac{n \text{ percent}}{100}$$

$3,600 \times n = 684 \times 100$

$n = 68,400 \div 3,600 = 19\%$

45. a.

$$\frac{\$n}{\$260} = \frac{20}{100}$$

$100 \times n = 20 \times 260$

$n = 5,200 \div 100 = \$52$

46. e.

$$\frac{\$1.79}{1 \text{ pound}} = \frac{\$1.06}{n \text{ pound}}$$

$1.79 \times n = 1 \times 1.06$

$n = 1.06 \div 1.79 = .59$ pound

47. b.

$$\frac{1\frac{1}{4} \text{ pound}}{\$7.80} = \frac{1 \text{ pound}}{\$n}$$

$\frac{5}{4} \times n = 7.80$

$n = 7.80 \times \frac{4}{5} = \$6.24$

48. a.

girder weight × number of girders = total weight

$\frac{7}{8}$ ton × 600 = 525 tons

49. c.

container size ÷ serving size = number of servings

9 pounds ÷ $\frac{1}{16}$ = 144 sundaes

50. b.

tile − size needed = size cut off

$\frac{3}{4}$ foot − $\frac{1}{3}$ foot = $\frac{5}{12}$ foot